the Story of Science

WeldonOwen
PUBLISHING

Published by
WeldonOwen Publishing
Ground Floor 42–44 Victoria Street, McMahons Point
Sydney NSW 2060, Australia
weldonowenpublishing.com

Copyright © 2012 Weldon Owen Pty Ltd

Managing Director Kay Scarlett
Publisher Corinne Roberts
Creative Director Sue Burk
Senior Vice President, International Sales Stuart Laurence
Sales Manager, North America Ellen Towell
Administration Manager, International Sales Kristine Ravn

Text Jack Challoner
Project Editor Scott Forbes
Designer Mark Thacker, Big Cat Design
Illustrator Dave Smith
Production Director Todd Rechner
Production and Prepress Controller Mike Crowton

ISBN 978-1-74252-280-7

Printed and bound in China by 1010 Printing Int Ltd
The paper used in the manufacture of this book
is sourced from wood grown in sustainable forests.
It complies with the Environmental Management System
Standard ISO 14001:2004

the Story of Science

AN ILLUSTRATED HISTORY

ATTENTION! this book skips the Boring Bits

WeldonOwen
PUBLISHING

Contents

Introduction 6

Episode 1 (1540s–1630s)

Earth moves! 7
Working out our place in space, with:
Nicolaus Copernicus • Johannes Kepler • Galileo Galilei

Episode 2 (1640s–1650s)

Thin air 11
Proving that nothing really does exist, and introducing:
Evangelista Torricelli • Otto von Guericke • Robert Boyle and Robert Hooke

Episode 3 (1660s–1670s)

Tiny things 14
Discovering a previously unseen realm, as revealed by:
Marcello Malpighi • Robert Hooke • Antony van Leeuwenhoek

Episode 4 (1670s–1680s)

On Earth as it is in the heavens 17
Seeking the laws that govern forces, assisted by:
Galileo Galilei • René Descartes • Isaac Newton

Episode 5 (1700s–1730s)

A particular matter 21
Finding out what everything is made of, featuring:
Democritus • Isaac Newton • Robert Boyle • Stephen Hales • Daniel Bernoulli

Episode 6 (1700s–1760s)

Fluid thinking 24
Investigating the mysteries of electricity, with:
William Gilbert • Francis Hauksbee • Stephen Gray
Abbé Jean-Antoine Nollet • Benjamin Franklin

Episode 7 (1710s–1780s)

A hot topic 28
Determining the nature of heat, in the company of:
Gabriel Fahrenheit • Anders Celsius • Joseph Black

Episode 8 (1750s–1790s)

Something in the air 31
Making sense of chemical reactions, assisted by:
George Stahl • Joseph Black • Henry Cavendish • Joseph Priestley
Antoine Lavoisier

Episode 9 (1780s–1800s)

Science in the landscape 35
Penetrating insights into the formation of Earth's crust, as set out by:
James Hutton • John Playfair

Episode 10 (1790s–1800s)

Progress, in tiny bits 38
Working out that everything really is made of atoms. Featuring:
Antoine Lavoisier • Luigi Galvani • Alessandro Volta • Joseph Proust • John Dalton

Episode 11 (1820s–1830s)

Making connections 41
How two forces became one, as established by:
Hans Christian Ørsted • André Ampère • Joseph Henry • Michael Faraday

Episode 12 (1820s–1850s)

Have you got the energy? 44
Discovering a unifying theory, in the company of:
Benjamin Thompson • Sadi Carnot • James Joule

Episode 13 (1830s–1860s)

The evolution of an idea 47
Revealing how species come and go, with:
Carolus Linnaeus • Charles Darwin

Episode 14 (1840s–1880s)

Light relief *50*

Probing the true nature of light, as revealed by:
Thomas Young • Hippolyte Fizeau • Michael Faraday • James Clerk Maxwell

Episode 15 (1860s)

An elementary system *53*

Revealing hidden patterns in chemistry, as identified by:
Gustav Kirchoff and Robert Bunsen • John Newlands • Dmitri Mendeleev

Episode 16 (1840s–1890s)

Wash your hands *56*

Finding out about germs, in the company of:
Ignaz Semmelweis • Louis Pasteur • Joseph Lister • Robert Koch

Episode 17 (1860s–1910s)

Smaller than atoms *60*

Exploring a new world of tiny particles, as unveiled by:
JJ Thomson • Marie Curie • Ernest Rutherford

Episode 18 (1900s–1910s)

Relatively revolutionary *63*

Adventures in time and space, starring:
Albert Einstein • Hermann Minkowski • Arthur Eddington

Episode 19 (1850s–1930s)

Pass it on *67*

Solving the mysteries of inheritance, thanks to:
Gregor Mendel • Walther Flemming • Walter Sutton • Thomas Hunt Morgan

Episode 20 (1900s–1920s)

How big is the Universe? *70*

Peering into deep, deep space, along with:
Friedrich Bessel • Henrietta Leavitt • Edwin Hubble

Episode 21 (1900s–1920s)

An uncertain world *73*

Weirdness on a small scale, as explained by:
Niels Bohr • Max Planck • Erwin Schrödinger

Episode 22 (1930s–1940s)

The particle zoo *76*

Discovering subatomic surprises in a hidden world, led by:
Paul Dirac • Carl Anderson • Hideki Yukawa • John Cockcroft and Ernest Walton

Episode 23 (1920s–1950s)

It's in the genes *79*

Unlocking the code of life, with keys supplied by:
Friedrich Miescher • Frederick Griffith • Rosalind Franklin
James Watson and Francis Crick

Episode 24 (1920s–1950s)

The origin of our species *83*

Locating the starting point of the human race, with:
Charles Darwin • Raymond Dart • Louis and Mary Leakey

Episode 25 (1910s–1960s)

A moving idea *85*

Working out how mountains and oceans are made, in the company of:
Alfred Wegener • Arthur Holmes • Harry Hess

Episode 26 (1920s–1960s)

Whispers from the Universe *88*

Looking back to the very beginning, alongside:
Georges Lemaître • Fred Hoyle • Arno Penzias and Robert Wilson

Episode 27 (from now on)

Science and progress *91*

Continuing the quest for knowledge – with a new generation of scientists.

Introduction

What is everything made of?
How do living things grow and reproduce?
How old is the universe? Why are there mountains?
Why are some things hotter than others?
Why do we get ill?
Questions like these lie at the very heart of science.

Curiosity – wondering about the world around us and trying to explain it – is part of being human. You might think, then, that science is as old as the human race. But science involves more than curiosity: it involves testing ideas about how the world works, with experiments, and rejecting an explanation if an experiment proves it to be wrong. People only started doing that a few hundred years ago.

There were some great thinkers in ancient civilisations, who pondered difficult questions and came up with explanations. But they didn't test their ideas. So our story does not begin then. The ancient explanations, particularly those from ancient Greece, were passed down through many generations and accepted by most people as facts. But in Europe during the 16th and 17th centuries, people began to question those old ideas, and soon they also began putting them to the test.

Just 400 years later, we have good, well-tested answers to the questions above, and many more besides. Of course, each answer brings more questions – but that's part of the fun. Science is a never-ending journey to truth, and the knowledge that scientists gain along the way can be put to good, or bad, use.

There is so much more to the history of science than we could ever fit in a book of this size. *The Story of Science* is like the highlights of a soccer match – focusing on the main events and weaving them together with commentary. But while soccer highlights compress 90 minutes of action into a few short minutes of video, this book compresses 500 years of people's inspiration and hard work into 27 short episodes.

Before we start . . .

- Most of the scientists mentioned in this book are white men. This is not because women or people of different ethnic origins are less clever or less important. It is just because of the way society used to be in Europe and America, which is where most of our story takes place. Today, there are many more female and non-white scientists, finding out amazing things, all over the world. After all, science is for everyone.

- A numbered 'century' always refers to the 100 years leading up to that number. So, for example, when you read that something happened 'in the 16th century', it means it happened between 1501 and 1600.

Earth moves!

Working out our place in space, with:

Nicolaus Copernicus, who realised Earth orbits the Sun (and not the other way round)

Johannes Kepler, who found the paths the planets follow

Galileo Galilei and his trusty telescope

The Sun, Moon and stars rise, cross the sky and set every day. From our viewpoint on Earth's surface, it looks like they move around us in great circles, and it feels like we are standing still. One of science's first successes was to prove that idea wrong – and to show that you can't always trust common sense.

Watch the night sky for years and you will see the same patterns of stars. It is as if the stars are 'fixed' onto a huge glass sphere that rotates around us once a day. But watch them carefully over even a few nights and you may notice that a few points of light change position relative to the fixed stars. These are planets (from the Greek word for 'wanderers').

The Ptolemaic system

Ancient people knew of five planets: Mercury, Venus, Mars, Jupiter and Saturn. Philosophers in ancient Greece suggested that the planets – and the Moon and Sun – must each be fixed to a separate transparent sphere, with Earth at the centre, each turning at a different speed.

However, the movements of the planets are not straightforward, and they were hard to explain. The planets move across the sky with varying speeds, and sometimes even change

Ptolemy shows off his model of the heavens – with Earth at the centre.

direction for a few weeks. The Greeks came up with a complicated system to account for these movements, while retaining the idea that Earth was stationary, at the centre of the universe. The 2nd-century astronomer Ptolemy explained the system in his book *Almagest*. This 'Ptolemaic' system could be used to predict the positions of the Sun, Moon and planets with reasonable accuracy – and it stuck. In Europe in the Middle Ages, the Catholic Church promoted it as if it were absolute truth – after all, even the Bible suggests that the Sun is moving, not Earth.

Copernicus's system in a book from 1600 – with the Sun at the centre

The Sun-centred universe

Early in the 16th century, when some scholars were questioning classical ideas, Polish astronomer Nicolaus Copernicus considered an alternative to the Ptolemaic system. He proposed that Earth was just one of several planets that orbit the Sun while rotating like a spinning top. In other words, the Earth was not the centre of the universe.

People had proposed this before, even in ancient Greece, but the notion had always been rejected. Copernicus explained the idea

Johannes Kepler with fellow astronomer Tycho Brahe (seated). You can't tell from this picture, but Tycho had a metal nose, because he lost his in a duel.

in a book called *De revolutionibus orbium coelestium (On the Revolution of the Heavenly Spheres)*. Realising it would be controversial, he delayed its publication for about 20 years, until 1543. Legend has it that he finally saw a printed copy of the book on the day he died.

The paths of the planets

The Catholic Church criticised Copernicus's book and removed it from circulation. But some open-minded people across Europe read it and realised that Copernicus's Sun-centred (heliocentric) system was more likely to be true than Ptolemy's Earth-centred (geocentric) system. One of them was a German mathematician and astronomer, Johannes Kepler.

The telescope

An exact replica of Galileo's telescope, through which he gazed at the night sky and changed our understanding of the universe.

Early 17th-century astronomers benefited from the invention of the telescope (a word that comes from the Greek words *tele*, meaning 'far away', and *skopein*, 'to look at'). The first telescopes were created by Dutch spectacle makers around 1600, when they realised that by combining two lenses they could make things appear about three times (3x) as big as they do to the naked eye. After learning about the new invention in 1609, Italian mathematician Galileo Galilei made his own 'Dutch glass', and improved the magnification to about 20x.

In 1600, Kepler began working for a Danish astronomer called Tycho Brahe. He was given access to detailed records that Brahe had kept of the movements of the planets. Kepler tried to match these movements with Copernicus's idea that the planets moved around the Sun in huge circular orbits, but, despite four years of painstaking and complicated calculations, he could not do so.

In 1605, however, he hit upon a new idea, something that no one had ever considered before: the planets' orbits might not be perfect circles. Indeed, Kepler's own observations suggested that the orbits followed a different shape: an oval, or ellipse. When he put that to the test, everything

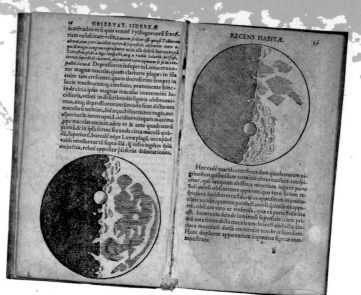

Galileo's sketches, in his book *The Starry Messenger* (1610).

fell into place. And once Kepler had shown that the planets follow elliptical orbits, astronomers found that they could predict the position of any planet at any time with incredible accuracy.

In the eyes of the beholder

In 1609, Italian mathematician Galileo Galilei became one of the first to raise a telescope to the night sky. He marvelled at mountains and craters on the Moon. And he found plenty of evidence in favour of a Sun-centred, not Earth-centred, universe, such as the moonlike phases of the planets Mercury and Venus, and four moons orbiting planet Jupiter. For many people, that settled the issue.

However, many others still held to the old Earth-centred idea. Importantly, the Roman Catholic Church remained opposed to the new theories. Throughout the 1620s, Galileo tried to persuade church leaders to change their minds. But when some of his ideas appeared to ridicule the old ways of thinking, the church took offence. In 1633, the Catholic authorities found Galileo guilty of heresy, put him under house arrest for the rest of his life and banned his books. Gradually, however, more and more people began to accept that Earth moves around the Sun – and that they were no longer at the centre of the universe.

One cardinal looks at Galileo's drawings while another checks out his telescope.

Thin air

Proving that nothing really does exist, and introducing:

Evangelista Torricelli, inventor of the barometer

Otto von Guericke and his experiments with vacuums

Robert Boyle and **Robert Hooke** and their improved vacuum pump

T he new ideas about space inspired many people, including German scientist and politician Otto von Guericke. Von Guericke was particularly interested in what lay between the planets and the stars. If it were air, wouldn't that air slow the planets in their orbits? Could it be that there was nothing there at all? In the new spirit of investigation, von Guericke set out to make empty space.

When von Guericke was a student, he had been taught the ideas of the ancient Greek philosopher Aristotle, who had argued that 'the void', or nothing, could not exist. Aristotle's thoughts were backed up by the observation that water and air quickly move to fill any space. However, an experiment carried out in 1643, by Italian scientist Evangelista Torricelli, had hinted that Aristotle might be wrong.

Mercury
– liquid at room temperature

Otto von Guericke

French scientist Blaise Pascal arranged for Torricelli's barometer to be taken up a mountain. As Pascal had predicted, the mercury column was shorter, because there is less air pushing down at altitude.

Creating space

While investigating air pressure, Torricelli poured mercury into a long glass tube that was sealed at the bottom. When he stood the tube upside down with the open end in a dish of mercury, some of the mercury in the tube slipped down into the dish. That left a space at the top that was free of air – a vacuum.

In 1647, inspired by Torricelli, von Guericke made (partial) vacuums by sucking air out of containers with a hand-held pump. After improving his pump, he carried out other experiments with vacuums, including proving that sound cannot pass through a vacuum, but light and magnetic force can.

Show of strength

In 1654, von Guericke staged a spectacular public demonstration in his hometown of Magdeburg. He held two copper hemispheres

'We live submerged at the bottom of an ocean of air.'
EVANGELISTA TORRICELLI, 1644

together to form a sphere 60 cm in diameter. He made the sphere airtight with leather and wax and evacuated the air from inside with his pump. With no air inside the sphere, there was no air pressure pressing outwards to balance the atmospheric pressure on the outside of the sphere – so the atmospheric pressure pushed the two hemispheres tightly together. Indeed, so tightly were the hemispheres pushed together that two rows of horses could not pull them apart. But when von Guericke opened the valve to let air back in, even a small child could easily separate them.

The following year in England, an Irish-born scientist, Robert Boyle, read about von Guericke's research, and set about designing an improved vacuum pump. His assistant, English scientist Robert Hooke, helped with the design and construction, and together they built a hand-cranked, piston-driven

Evangelista Torricelli invents the barometer

Torricelli investigated air pressure to find out why water pumps and siphons could raise water no more than 10 m, as several people had noted. He thought it was the weight of the atmosphere pressing down on the main body of water below that pushed the water up the tube, and that a 10-m column was the most this 'atmospheric pressure' could support. Experimenting with his tube of mercury, a much more dense liquid, he found the atmospheric pressure would support a column only 76 cm tall. He then noted that the height of the mercury changed with the weather, as the pressure varied. Torricelli had invented the first barometer – an instrument still used to measure atmospheric pressure.

pump that was much more powerful. Since then, vacuum pumps have proved vital in many important scientific discoveries – including the invention of the light bulb and the television.

Von Guericke's demonstration of the power of atmospheric pressure, which is stronger than eight horses.

Replica of Boyle's vacuum pump. In use, it would have had a glass jar on top; turning the handle pumped the air out of the jar.

Tiny things

Discovering a previously unseen realm, as revealed by:

Marcello Malpighi, first to see blood vessels

Robert Hooke, who made beautiful drawings of minuscule creatures

Antony van Leeuwenhoek, discoverer of microorganisms

Hooke's drawings of 'cells' in a cork.

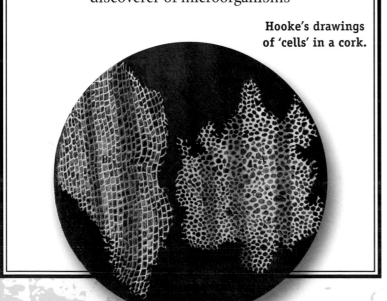

Robert Hooke, the assistant who helped construct the first mechanical vacuum pump, was also a pioneer of microscopy – making and using microscopes. The microscope allowed people to see things in new ways, to challenge outdated beliefs – and to investigate tiny things that no one had ever seen before.

The second half of the 17th century was an exciting time in microscopy. In 1661, for example, Italian scientist Marcello Malpighi became the first person to see blood capillaries. This was groundbreaking. Almost 40 years earlier, English physician William Harvey had challenged an ancient idea by suggesting that blood circulates. Harvey thought, correctly, that blood is pumped out from the heart, travels out through arteries and back to the heart through veins. In 1628, he carried out an experiment that seemed to confirm the idea. But until Malpighi saw the capillaries, no one had been able to find any physical connection between the arteries and the veins.

A flea as depicted in Hooke's book

Peering into another world

The word 'microscope' is based on the Greek words *micron* (small) and *skopein* (look at). The compound microscope – one with two or more lenses – was invented in the 1590s, when Dutch spectacle makers put two lenses together in an arrangement that made things look several times bigger. By the 1650s, scientists were routinely looking at things through microscopes, but the magnification was limited to about 10x. In the late 1650s, Robert Hooke improved the design, enabling microscopes with shorter tubes and higher magnification – up to about 30x.

Hooke's microscope

The opening pages of Hooke's scientific bestseller, *Micrographia*, published in 1665.

In 1665, Hooke published a remarkable book called *Micrographia*, which contained his own stunning drawings of the things he had seen when gazing through his microscope tube. One of the things he described was the soft wood cork – 'all perforated and porous, much like a honeycomb' – and he came up with a word to describe the spaces in the cork: 'cells'. In 1668, Dutch microscopist Jan Swammerdam observed what he called 'globules' in blood, thereby becoming the first person ever to see red blood cells.

A world in a raindrop

In the 1670s, another Dutch man made more startling discoveries using a microscope. Cloth

Mr Hooke takes a close look at fleas

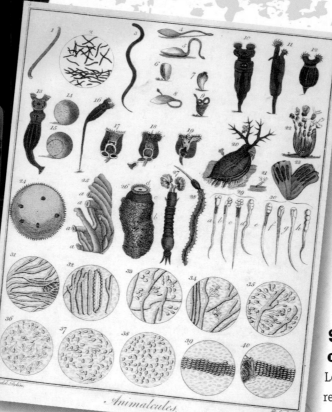

Animalcules.

Sightings confirmed

Leeuwenhoek wrote repeatedly to the most prestigious scientific organisation of the day, the Royal Society, in London, England, to tell them about the animalcules and other things he had seen. Members of the Royal Society were sceptical at first, as were most other scientists in Europe – no one else had microscopes anywhere near as powerful as Leeuwenhoek's. For followers of the new approach to finding out about the world known as science, it was important for discoveries to be verified. So, the Royal Society gave Hooke the task of confirming Leeuwenhoek's claims, and after a month of trying, and several improvements to his microscope, he saw the same things.

In the next few decades, microscopes improved in magnification and clarity, and incredible new discoveries in biology came thick and fast. But it would be another 150 years before scientists realised that cells like the ones that Hooke, Swammerdam and Leeuwenhoek had observed are the basic unit of all living things.

merchant Antony van Leeuwenhoek had been familiar with strong magnifying glasses, which he used to examine woven fabrics. Inspired by Hooke's *Micrographia*, he set out to make a really powerful microscope. Unlike most other people's microscopes, which had two lenses, Leeuwenhoek's had a single lens – a tiny glass bead that he ground himself and fixed to a handheld brass mount. His microscope had a magnification of nearly 300x – around ten times as powerful as Hooke's.

In 1674, Leeuwenhoek, too, saw red 'globules' (cells) in blood – he estimated their size at around $\frac{1}{2,500}$ the diameter of a grain of sand. And in 1675, in a sample of pond water, he saw tiny living things far too small to be seen with the naked eye. He had become the first person ever to see microorganisms, which he called 'animalcules'. He also saw them in rainwater, in spit and later in plaque he scraped from teeth, and estimated (correctly) that there are several million in a single raindrop.

'I then most always saw, with great wonder, that in the said matter there were many very little living animalcules, very prettily a-moving.'

ANTONY VAN LEEUWENHOEK, 1683

On Earth
as it is in the heavens

Seeking the laws that govern forces, assisted by:

Galileo Galilei and his theories of friction

René Descartes' coordinate system

Isaac Newton's three laws of motion

At the same time as he was investigating Leeuwenhoek's 'animalcules', Robert Hooke was pondering big questions about the Solar System. In 1679, Hooke wrote to Isaac Newton, a professor of mathematics at Cambridge University, England, asking if Newton had any thoughts about what keeps the planets in their orbits.

Understanding how things move had long been a major preoccupation of scientists and philosophers. In ancient Greece, Aristotle had declared that an object only moves when a force (a push or a pull) is acting on it; when the force stops, the movement stops. The 'free' movement of projectiles – like balls thrown through the air – didn't fit this explanation though: nothing is pushing on them once they have left your hand. But Aristotle had an

Galileo working out how gravity can speed objects down slopes – and scare assistants

answer to that: air rushes into the space behind a projectile and the moving air pushes the projectile, keeping it moving.

Motion and friction

In the Middle Ages, Islamic and European philosophers adjusted Aristotle's ideas slightly. They suggested that when things are pushed to start them moving, they are given a certain amount of 'impetus', which gradually runs out, so that things eventually stop moving. But they were wrong – and so was Aristotle.

At the beginning of the 17th century, Galileo experimented with forces and motion. In particular, he was fascinated by how forces cause objects to speed up and slow down. To work out how gravity causes things to speed up, he allowed balls to roll down different slopes, carefully timing how long the balls took to reach the bottom. Galileo found that without any force acting, moving objects continue to move at the same speed and in the same direction. Motion does not 'run out', and motion does not stop when the force stops – in fact, a force is needed to make a moving object stop. Galileo introduced the concepts of friction and air resistance, forces that slow things down. In everyday life, things tend to stop moving because of the force of friction, not because they run out of impetus or the air stops pushing them.

Predicting by numbers

The question Hooke had asked Newton – about what keeps the planets in their orbits – had become very important now that it was clear that Earth itself moves. In the 1630s, French philosopher René Descartes suggested that planets were pushed along by a maelstrom of closely packed, swirling particles. Despite that idea being wrong, Descartes is a very significant figure in the history of science.

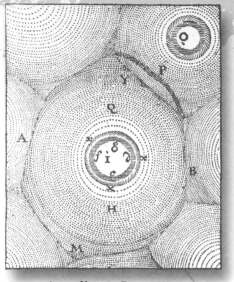

According to Descartes, swirling vortices pushed planets around the Sun.

One of his most important contributions was a way of representing the position of an object with numbers, a system now known as Cartesian coordinates. This allowed scientists to express the motion of objects as equations; as a result, theories about force and motion could be represented by equations, too. In this way, scientists could make precise predictions of objects' motions, and comparing the predictions with the outcomes of experiments allowed them to test their theories.

Motion and gravity

The work of Descartes and Galileo had a profound influence on young Isaac Newton. In 1666, while he was studying at Cambridge University, Newton had to move to his family home for a few months, to escape a plague epidemic that had hit London and Cambridge. And it was there, at home, that Newton made most of his important discoveries.

As a brilliant mathematician, Newton was able to express his new observations and ideas about force and motion mathematically, using equations as well as geometry. In fact, Newton managed to explain the movements of all objects with just three 'laws'. The first was Galileo's discovery that an object's motion

Scientists wondered: what keeps the Moon from flying off into space?

continues unless a force acts on the object. The second law stated that when a force acts, it causes an object to accelerate (change its speed and/or direction) by an amount that depends upon the mass of the object and the strength and direction of the force. And the third law stated that for every force, there is another force of equal strength in the opposite direction. Using these simple laws, scientists could predict the motion of any object at any time.

Also in 1666, Newton made the connection between what makes things fall downwards on Earth and what keeps planets in their orbits. He realised that gravity – the force that keeps your feet on the ground – pulls objects

A 19th-century portrait of **Isaac Newton**

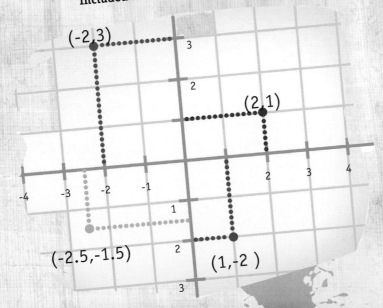

Using Descartes' coordinate system, the positions of objects can be described with numbers and, in turn, included in mathematical equations.

(-2,3)

(2,1)

(-2.5,-1.5)

(1,-2)

together, even across space. The strength of the force depends upon the masses of the objects and how far apart they are, a relationship that can be expressed as an equation.

The equation not only predicted the motion of falling objects, but also the orbits of the planets around the Sun and the Moon around Earth. The new theory of gravitation fitted perfectly with Kepler's observations about the planets' orbits: the fact that planetary orbits are ellipses was hidden in Newton's equation. And it is indeed gravity that keeps the Moon in orbit – the same force that keeps us in our seats and makes a stone or any other projectile fall to the ground.

Newton imagined a cannonball shot horizontally from a mountaintop with enough speed to go around the planet, always falling towards the ground but following the curve of the planet's surface and never reaching the ground. Just like that projectile, the Moon is constantly falling towards us but never reaches the ground. If the Moon stopped moving, it would accelerate downwards like any other falling object, and crash into Earth. Similarly, if you could turn off gravity, the Moon would move off in a straight line at a constant speed until some other force acted on it.

Universal laws

So, in 1679, when Hooke asked Newton if he had any thoughts about the planets' orbits, Newton had lots to say and wrote Hooke a long series of letters. In 1686, he set out all of his mathematical laws of force, motion and gravity, and the details of his experiments, in a book called *Philosophiæ Naturalis Principia Mathematica (Mathematical Principles of Natural Philosophy)* – the *Principia* for short – which was published in 1686.

The fact that the same force is responsible for the behaviour of the Moon, Earth or a cannonball meant that Newton's law of gravitation is a 'universal' law. His laws of motion, too, were universal. The power of science to reduce complicated motion to a few simple rules was impressive, and soon more and more people began to join the quest to measure, observe and understand the universe.

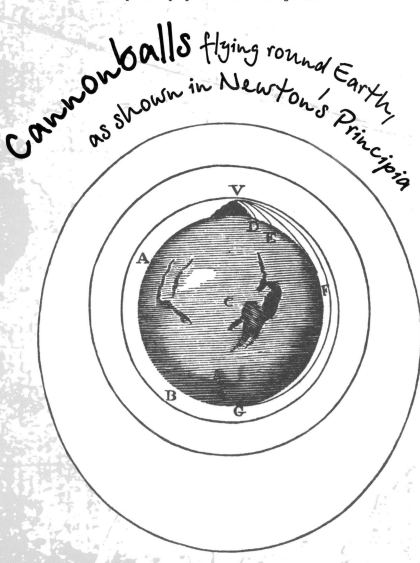

Cannonballs flying round Earth, as shown in Newton's Principia

'This grand book, the universe, continually open to our gaze...is written in the language of mathematics.' GALILEO, 1623

A particular matter

Finding out what everything is made of, featuring:

Democritus, who coined the term 'atom'

Isaac Newton's particles

Robert Boyle and the elasticity of air

Stephen Hales' expanding gases

Daniel Bernoulli's clear view of gases

An essential part of the new picture of the universe painted by Newton was the idea that matter is made of tiny particles that are governed by the same laws that move the planets. Thinking of matter as particles helped make sense of von Guericke's vacuums. If particles and empty space are all there is, then removing the particles leaves just empty space – a vacuum, in other words.

The smallest parts

One of the first people to think that matter might be made of tiny particles was the

Democritus was one of the first to ponder the smallest of things.

ancient Greek philosopher Democritus, who lived more than 2,000 years before Newton. Democritus wondered what would happen if you kept cutting an object in half and in half again. Could you keep doing that forever, making ever smaller pieces? Or would you end up with a 'smallest part', something you could not cut in half? Democritus referred to those smallest parts as 'atoms', from the Greek word *atomos*, which means 'cannot be divided'. For hundreds of years, most philosophers and scientists had rejected Democritus's idea. But Newton's laws made it popular once again – at least for a while.

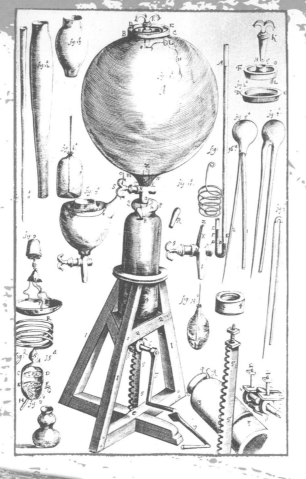

Boyle used his trusty vacuum pump in his investigation of air, and his discovery of Boyle's law.

In his 1704 book *Opticks*, Newton offered explanations of some everyday phenomena in terms of the particles of matter, including explanations of sound and heat. He also suggested that light is a stream of particles. It is amazing to think of a drop of water or a pinhead – in fact, everything around you – as being made up of billions of moving particles, far too small to see. It is perhaps even more amazing to imagine Newton thinking that, too, more than 300 years ago.

The nature of air

As Newton saw it, the particles in solids and liquids must strongly attract each other (pull together). This would explain why these forms of matter don't spread out as gases do. At the time, scientists didn't distinguish between gases and referred to all forms of gas as simply 'air'. Even though 'air' was invisible, Newton

True colours

The main subject of Newton's book *Opticks* was light and colour. Newton thought that light must be a stream of particles, which bounce off shiny objects and deviate as they pass through transparent objects like glass lenses. But he couldn't explain how light particles could be different colours. In the most famous experiment in *Opticks*, Newton used a glass prism to split white light into its spectrum of colours. By doing this, Newton showed that white light, rather than being a pure light as people then believed it to be, is actually a mixture of colours.

and many other scientists of his day thought that it, too, would be made of particles.

Back in the 1660s, Robert Boyle had experimented with air, investigating how it pushes back – how its pressure increases, in other words – when it is compressed. This property of a substance – to push back when it is squashed (or pull back when it is stretched) – is called 'elasticity'. Air is much more elastic than, say, stone. Boyle found a simple law to describe the elasticity of air. It states that if you squash air to half its volume, the air pressure doubles; squash it to one-third of its volume and the pressure triples; at one-quarter of the volume, the pressure quadruples – and so on. As a result of Boyle's Law, scientists began to refer to air as an 'elastic fluid' (a fluid is anything that flows: a liquid or a gas). Newton imagined the tiny particles of air as stationary balls connected by springs.

A space filler

In the 1720s, English amateur scientist Stephen Hales made a startling discovery about air. He heated up plant and animal matter – as well as non-living (inorganic) matter – and also carried out various chemical reactions. In each case, he collected the 'air' that apparently escaped from the matter under investigation. When he heated just 1 cubic inch of honey, for example (about 16 cm³), 'there arose 144 cubic inches of air'.

Hales concluded that most solids and liquids held huge amounts of air, pushing to get out, and that heat or chemical action would allow it to escape. Once out, the air would expand to fill any space and would exert pressure as normal. His results appeared in his book *Vegetable Staticks*, which was published in 1727. They fitted neatly with the idea of air as an elastic fluid.

Stephen Hales
releasing 'air' from honey

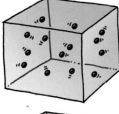
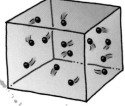

How Bernoulli pictured free-moving air particles, at low temperature (top) and moving faster when heated (above).

Flying free

In the 1730s, Swiss mathematician Daniel Bernoulli came up with a different vision of how the particles of air behave. Bernoulli suggested that instead of the particles being stationary and repelling each other, they might be free of each other, flying around at speed in all directions. Then the pressure of the air would be the result of the collisions of the particles against the sides of a container. In 1738, Bernoulli used Newton's laws to construct an equation that calculated the average speed of air particles. This equation could also be used to estimate air pressure at different temperatures. The equation really worked, and Bernoulli's idea is close to the modern understanding of a gas. It was a remarkable achievement. But Bernoulli was ahead of his time: it was Newton's idea – that the particles of air were stationary and repelled each other – that persisted.

Fluid thinking

Investigating the mysteries of electricity, with:

William Gilbert, first to call electricity a fluid

Francis Hauksbee's electrifying globe

Stephen Gray and his human conductors

Abbé Jean-Antoine Nollet and his shocking experiments

Benjamin Franklin's dangerous kite trick

Floating in water, a magnetised needle stuck in a cork is free to line up with Earth's magnetic forces.

Stephen Hales thought he had found evidence that air was squashed inside ordinary matter, pushing to get out. As the 18th century continued, scientists came to believe that a similar invisible, elastic fluid might be behind the phenomenon of electricity. For how else could they explain those invisible forces that made objects attract and repel, caused hairs to stand on end and created sparks?

English physician William Gilbert was the first to suggest electricity might be a kind of fluid, in his 1600 book *De Magnete (All About Magnetism)*. Gilbert experimented with amber (fossilised tree resin). Rubbing amber with fur causes both materials to become electrically charged – in the same way as rubbing a party balloon in your hair makes the balloon and the hair charged. Charged amber and fur attract each other and they both attract other objects, such as pieces of hair and paper. People had noticed that some materials behave in this way as far back as ancient Greece.

Gilbert believed the electric fluid existed inside substances like amber and the fur. He imagined that when he rubbed these substances, the fluid expanded and surrounded the object, like the atmosphere around Earth. As the fluid 'fell' back into the object, it pulled small objects with it. Gilbert did not notice that electricity could repel as well as attract. But in 1628 Italian scientist Niccolò Cabeo found that if you bring two pieces of charged amber – or two pieces of charged fur – close to each other, they push apart.

Highly charged

The 18th century was the heyday of experimental science, and electricity became a favourite subject of investigation. In 1706, English scientist Francis Hauksbee realised that by rubbing glass on skin he could generate electricity, so he mounted a glass globe on an axle attached to a hand crank. When he rested one hand on the glass while turning the globe rapidly with the other, electrical crackles could be heard – the globe had become highly charged. Thereafter, it would attract objects and could be used to charge other things to be used in experiments.

Soon, Hauksbee's globe became a standard piece of equipment. Scientists imagined that charging an object meant they were forcing more fluid into it – indeed, the word 'charged' means 'filled'. The idea that the fluid could leak out again helped explain how charged objects could exert a force over distances.

Another elastic fluid

William Gilbert was the first person to write about electrical forces, and in *De Magnete* he used the word *electricus*, meaning 'like amber'. The word came from *electron*, the Greek word for amber, and Gilbert's word is the source of the word 'electricity'. However, as the title of his book suggests, Gilbert was mostly interested in magnetism. He suggested that Earth has an iron core that acts like a huge magnet, and he catalogued the behaviour of magnets and magnetic substances. For some time after, the origin of magnetic forces remained just as much a mystery as the origin of electrical forces – 18th-century scientists experimented with magnets, too, and they thought of magnetism as another elastic fluid, just like electricity.

Hauksbee's globe. Turn the handle, rest a hand on the spinning globe, and sparks will soon fly.

Electric circuit

Perhaps the most important piece of apparatus for scientists who were studying electricity was the Leyden jar. This was a glass jar with metal foil coating on the outside and on the inside. The foil inside was connected to a metal rod, which the experimenter would touch with an electrically charged object to charge up the jar. Leyden jars could store large amounts of electric charge, which the experimenters could release with dramatic effect. Using a Leyden jar, French scientist Abbé Jean-Antoine Nollet carried out a spectacular variation of Gray's demonstration. As entertainment for the king of France, Nollet gave simultaneous electric shocks to 180 royal guards, who were holding hands in a circle – all of whom jumped and gasped at the same time.

A Leyden jar. A metal chain connects the top metal knob with the foil inside the jar.

In the 1720s, English physicist Stephen Gray observed that some materials seemed to allow 'electric fluid' to pass through them, while others did not. Four years later, French-born scientist John Desaguliers gave them the names we use today: 'conductors', which convey electricity, and 'insulators', which do not. Like many experimental scientists of the day, Gray frequently gave public demonstrations. He found that by carefully choosing conductors and insulators for different parts of his apparatus, he could gain control over electrical effects. One demonstration, copied by many other scientists of the day, involved a boy suspended from silk threads. When Gray touched the boy's legs with a charged glass rod, the boy's hands and face could attract pieces of paper. Electric charge had passed along or through the boy's body, but could not escape through the silk, an insulator.

The Leyden jar reinforced the idea of electricity as a fluid: what better way to store a fluid than in a jar? It also made it possible to produce impressive sparks – a source of fascination to electrical researchers. Sparks also reinforced the idea of electricity as a fluid, and made people think of the fluid as a kind of fire. In 1784, Dutch scientist Martinus van Marum made a machine that produced a spark 60 cm long and about 3 mm thick.

Courting danger

In 1752, American statesman Benjamin Franklin carried out a celebrated but dangerous experiment. He flew a silk kite in the air during a thunderstorm, to test the idea that lightning is an electrical phenomenon. He found he could collect electric charge and use it to do all the experiments he would normally do with electricity generated by rubbing fur on amber. Other scientists died trying to replicate Franklin's experiment – it is not a good idea to fly a kite in a thunderstorm!

'And when the rain has wet the kite and the twine, so that it can conduct the electric fire freely, you will find it stream out plentifully from the key on the approach of your knuckle.'

BENJAMIN FRANKLIN, 1752

The electrical experiments and demonstrations were impressive. But there were few clues as to the real nature of electricity, and there was a lot of confusion and disagreement. For example, Benjamin Franklin believed that there was a single electrical fluid, and thought that things became charged if they had too much of it (creating a positive charge) or too little (a negative charge). Abbé Nollet thought there were two different fluids. The scientists of the 18th century made little real progress in understanding what was behind the phenomena associated with electricity. However, picturing electricity as a fluid gave scientists something to measure, and something to debate.

Nollet used shock tactics to impress the French royal family.

A hot topic

Determining the nature of heat, in the company of:

Gabriel Fahrenheit, inventor of the mercury thermometer

Anders Celsius, creator of the Celsius scale

Joseph Black, who went hunting for hidden heat

Galileo's thermometer wasn't a true thermometer, because it had no scale to measure temperature.

Isaac Newton, Robert Boyle and a few other scientists had suspected that heat is the motion of the particles of matter: the more vigorously an object's particles move, the hotter the object is. But many people in the 18th century weren't convinced that matter is made of particles. Most scientists considered heat – like electricity and magnetism – as another invisible fluid that could be 'contained' in objects and could pass from one to another.

Measuring temperature

In 1592 Galileo made the first form of thermometer – the word is based on the Greek words *thermos* (hot) and *metron* (measure). It indicated changes in temperature but, having no scale, didn't actually 'measure' anything. In the 17th century, however, people started adding scales to their thermometers, to measure 'degrees of heat', and in 1714 Swedish physicist and glassblower Gabriel Fahrenheit invented the first accurate thermometer, which consisted of mercury in a sealed glass tube and had a simple degree scale.

In 1732, Dutch scientist Herman Boerhaave suggested that temperature is the concentration of heat fluid: cram more heat fluid into the same space, and the temperature rises. This made sense of mixing substances at different temperatures. For example, mix a cup of water at 40 degrees with one at 50 degrees, and the final temperature will be 45 degrees. But in the 1740s, Fahrenheit carried out experiments that challenged

Boerhaave's simple idea. Fahrenheit mixed two identical amounts of water and mercury at different temperatures. This time, the resulting temperature was much closer to the water's temperature, rather than halfway between the two. Fahrenheit also placed a cup of water and a cup of mercury next to a fire; the mercury heated up more quickly. It seemed that different substances were able to hold different amounts of heat fluid – or at least absorb it at different rates.

Latent heat

Scottish chemist Joseph Black referred to the ability of a substance to hold heat as its 'heat capacity'. As a chemist, he was comfortable thinking of heat as a substance or fluid, and the idea of heat capacity made sense. It simply meant that some substances react more strongly with heat fluid, or bind more tightly to it – just as, for example, you can dissolve more sugar in water than you can in vegetable oil.

However, Black went on to make an important discovery that should perhaps have put the existence of heat fluid in doubt. In 1761, he measured how much heat a block of ice absorbs while it is melting and found that it was enough to increase the temperature of water by about 78°C. And yet the temperature

'I imagined that, during the boiling, heat is absorbed by the water, and enters into the composition of the vapour produced.'

JOSEPH BLACK, 1760

Temperature scales

In the 18th century, dozens of scientists invented temperature scales, each defined by different 'fixed points', so that anyone using them would come up with the same number for the same temperature. Two of these scales survive today, though in slightly altered form. In 1724 Fahrenheit created a scale using the coldest mixture scientists could make – ice, water, salt and ammonium chloride – as 0 degrees and, curiously, the body temperature of a horse as his 100-degree fixed point. In 1742, Swedish astronomer Anders Celsius invented a scale with 100 degrees between the temperatures of melting ice and boiling water. Oddly, Celsius designed it with boiling water at 0 degrees and melting ice at 100 degrees; another Swedish scientist, Carl Linnaeus, reversed it in 1744, the year Celsius died.

Heat as an element

We now know that heat is not a fluid, and that the extra heat absorbed by melting ice or boiling water is required to break particles free from each other. But the idea of heat as a fluid, a particular substance, held sway for some time. In 1784, French chemist Antoine Lavoisier even gave it a name, caloric (*calorique* in French), and included it in his list of chemical elements. In fact, it was not until the 1850s that scientists worked out the real nature of heat and temperature – and showed that Newton and Boyle had been onto something after all.

Joseph Black was determined to find out where the latent heat was hiding.

of the ice remains unchanged while it melts – it doesn't 'heat up' at all. In 1762, he made a similar measurement for boiling water, which stays at the same temperature until it has all vaporised to become steam; in this case, the boiling water absorbed enough heat to raise the temperature by more than 440°C.

Scientists had assumed that, as a physical substance, heat fluid could not be created or destroyed, only transferred from one place to another. So what happened to the heat that went missing in the melting ice and boiling water? To Black, the heat fluid was still there, but it was bound strongly to the steam or the water – 'hidden' from the thermometer. He therefore called this hidden heat 'latent heat' (latent means hidden).

Antoine Lavoisier and (left) his ice calorimeter, a device he invented in 1782 to measure the heat produced in chemical reactions.

Something in the air

Making sense of chemical reactions, assisted by:

Georg Stahl and the phlogiston theory

Joseph Black, first to isolate carbon dioxide

Henry Cavendish, discoverer of hydrogen

Joseph Priestley's 'dephlogisticated air'

Antoine Lavoisier and his pioneering chemical experiments

Fanciful image of alchemist c. 1600

The 18th-century experiments with heat and electricity were exciting and thought provoking, but they hadn't taken scientists much closer to discovering the true nature of heat and electricity. At the end of the century, however, the rapid development of the science of chemistry led to more significant progress.

Chemistry is the study of what substances are made of and how they change in chemical reactions. The predecessor of the science of chemistry was a mystical art called alchemy. Across much of the ancient world, alchemists burned, mixed and distilled substances, hoping to gain control over the transformation of matter. In the process, medieval Arabic alchemists developed many of the techniques used in chemistry laboratories today.

Early European scientists took to alchemy enthusiastically, but the procedures used by alchemists did not follow the scientific method. In 1661, however, in his influential book, *The Sceptical Chymist*, Robert Boyle suggested that the mysteries of chemical reactions could be solved by observing, weighing and measuring. The adoption of this more scientific approach would eventually spell the end of alchemy, and the beginning of the science of chemistry.

The phlogiston theory

One of the most important ingredients in the alchemist's laboratory was fire, which could bring about or speed up chemical reactions. In 1703, German scientist Georg Stahl suggested that combustible (burnable) materials contain

Most alchemists had two main aims: to turn ordinary dull metals into gold and to produce a kind of medicine called an elixir that would cure all ills and make a person live forever. These two aims were related: gold is inert (unreactive) and so does not corrode; it lasts forever. An elixir, it was hoped, would give people the same property. When scientists in Europe adopted the aims and practices of alchemy, they came to believe that a single substance, referred to as the Philosopher's Stone, could achieve both aims.

Joseph Wright's 1771 painting shows Hennig Brand searching for the Philosopher's Stone - and finding phosphorus.

Searching for a miraculous substance

an invisible substance called 'phlogiston', which would be released when such a material is burned, leaving other materials behind. According to this theory, for example, wood consisted of ash and phlogiston – when wood was burned, the phlogiston was released and the ash left behind.

The followers of the phlogiston theory proposed that air is needed to absorb phlogiston; this explained why things don't burn in a vacuum, as Boyle had shown. They also asserted that air can only absorb a certain amount of phlogiston – that explained why a candle will only burn for a short time in a sealed jar. Odd as it may seem to us today, the theory was very popular in the 18th century.

Breaking down the elements

Since ancient times, most alchemists and philosophers had assumed that fire was

an element – a pure substance that can't be broken down into simpler substances – and that everything was made of just four elements: earth, air, fire and water. Ash, for example, would be mostly earth. The alchemists liked this idea, because it suggested that any type of matter could in theory be changed or 'transmuted' into any other, just by changing the amount of each element. But the idea of the four elements was thrown into doubt in the 1660s, when German alchemist Hennig Brand discovered a previously unknown substance, which he called 'phosphorus'. Brand's substance was not air, earth, fire or water but it was an element: it could not be broken down.

The four elements theory took another knock in 1751, when Joseph Black found that air is not an element at all: it is actually a mixture of substances. Black had been

Henry Cavendish,

discoverer of 'inflammable air' which we now call hydrogen

Six years later, Swedish chemist Carl Wilhelm Scheele discovered yet another new air. He called it 'fire air', because things burned very well in it. Today, we call it oxygen. Scheele produced the new air by heating a red powder called mercury calx (mercuric oxide). English scientist Joseph Priestley discovered the same air independently, in the same way, two years later. Priestley found that mice lived much longer in a jar of the new air than in ordinary air. He even breathed it himself, noting that his chest 'felt peculiarly light and easy for some time afterwards'. He called the new air 'dephlogisticated air'. To Priestley, the reason why things burned so well in it was that it had had its phlogiston removed – and could therefore reabsorb it readily.

investigating 'magnesia alba', a chemical that was used to treat indigestion – today we call it magnesium carbonate. When heated or mixed with an acid, magnesia alba releases a gas. At this time, of course, all gases were referred to as 'air'. But Black realised that the air released by magnesia alba was part of, but different from, normal air, and proved this with a series of ingenious tests. He found, for example, that animals could not survive in the new air, and that it extinguished a flame. What he had isolated was, in fact, carbon dioxide.

Air within air

In 1766, English scientist Henry Cavendish discovered another 'air', after collecting the bubbles produced when metals slowly dissolved in acids. Cavendish's new air burned extremely well, with a loud pop. Cavendish thought he might have actually collected phlogiston itself. He called it 'inflammable air'; today, we call it hydrogen. Cavendish also noticed that when he burned inflammable air it produced droplets of water – but he couldn't explain why.

Joseph Priestley's mouse enjoys the benefits of dephlogisticated air.

Chemical reactions observed

In 1774, Priestley travelled to France. While he was there, he explained his discovery to leading chemist Antoine Lavoisier, who was by then widely known for his extremely precise experiments. Lavoisier immediately repeated Priestley's and Scheele's experiment, and he was struck by an idea: that burning was a chemical reaction, in which Priestley's dephlogisticated air joined, or bonded, with other elements. He named dephlogisticated air 'oxygen', and proved his theory correct in a brilliant set of experiments. Lavoisier also made sense of Cavendish's observation that burning inflammable air produces drops of water. He realised that when inflammable air burned, it combined with oxygen from the air. Lavoisier called inflammable air 'hydrogen', which means 'water maker'. He even managed to get hydrogen out of water, by 'decomposing' hot steam.

Lavoisier had made sense of chemical reactions scientifically for the first time, and had become the first to understand the true meaning of elements (like oxygen and hydrogen), compounds (like water) and chemical reactions – the joining and separating of different elements. Alchemy and the quest to find the Philosopher's Stone were dead. And the theories of phlogiston and the four elements were dead, too. But the new science of chemistry was alive and well.

Antoine Lavoisier experimenting with burning, or combustion, in 1774, using a huge burning mirror. Note the sunglasses.

'We ought, in every instance, to submit our reasoning to the test of experiment, and never to search for truth but by the natural road of experiment and observation.'

ANTOINE LAVOISIER, 1790

Science
in the landscape

Penetrating insights into the formation of Earth's crust, as set out by:

James Hutton, who read the ages of the rocks

John Playfair, who explained it all better

Mr Hutton! rock star

C hemistry was not the only activity that became a science towards the end of the 18th century. Another was geology, the study of rocks and the landscape. And just as the insight and careful observations of Antoine Lavoisier made chemistry into a true science, so the birth of geology as a science was largely down to one person: Scottish amateur scientist James Hutton.

Geology aims to answer questions like 'How old is Earth?', 'How do mountains form?' and 'What is it like deep beneath our feet?' James Hutton was fascinated by questions like these, and he realised the importance of observation in answering them. Consequently, Hutton became as familiar with the landscape of his native Scotland as Lavoisier was with chemical reactions.

'The past history of our globe must be explained by what can be seen to be happening now.'

JAMES HUTTON, 1785

An everchanging scene

When he was in his twenties, Hutton lived on a farm. He observed over months and years how rain washed soil off the land into rivers, and he realised that the rivers were carrying the soil to the ocean, where doubtless it sank to the seabed. He also realised that rain and rivers slowly erode rocks, too, carrying them away tiny bit by tiny bit. Hutton surmised that if this process carried on for long enough, there would be many layers of sediment on the seafloor, and that the weight of the layers would squash the lower ones, forming 'sedimentary rocks'. Hutton saw these rock layers all around him – but they were above the level of the sea. It became clear that some huge force must have thrust them out of the ocean and that volcanoes and earthquakes might have something to do with it.

Not all the rocks were layered, however: others looked as if they had once been molten (liquid). Some of these 'frozen' rocks had large crystals in them, while others had small ones. Hutton deduced that for crystals to grow large those rocks must have cooled and solidified slowly, whereas rocks with smaller crystals must have solidified more quickly. Some had no crystals at all and appeared like glass;

Volcanoes provided James Hutton with evidence of Earth's internal heat, which was central to his theory.

These layers of sedimentary rocks have been tilted upwards by immense forces.

like glass, they must have solidified very quickly, before any crystals could form.

Hutton knew that there was molten rock in volcanoes, and imagined the planet might have a molten core. He realised that molten rock flowing out of volcanoes could seep into cracks in surrounding rocks and melt those rocks, and that once the volcano became dormant the molten rock would cool slowly, forming large crystals. There are plenty of dormant volcanoes in Scotland, and the rocks around them fitted with Hutton's ideas.

The age of the world

Hutton began to build up a picture of how Earth works. He came to understand that the planet is continuously changing. The landscape erodes, making sedimentary rocks, which may then be lifted and folded by tremendous forces, or melted by heat from volcanoes. Meanwhile, molten rock from volcanoes is also forming new rock, even under the sea, where it adds to the ocean floor.

It became clear, too, to Hutton that these processes must have taken a very, very long time – and that Earth must be extremely old. But that was completely different from what he had been taught. In late 18th-century Europe, the Bible was the authority on how Earth and the landscape had formed, and from biblical evidence several scholars had calculated the age of Earth as only about 6,000 years. The most 'accurate' date given for the creation of our planet came from English bishop James Ussher; in 1654, he carefully worked out that God must have created the world on the evening of 22 October 4004 BCE. What is more, the Bible stated that God made Earth pretty much as it is – that it wasn't changing. Geologists of the day tended to believe that sedimentary rocks they saw in the landscape had all been formed during the great flood described in the Bible (during which Noah built his ark), and that even the rocks with tiny crystals had formed then.

Ideas overturned

Hutton knew his ideas would be controversial, so he looked for more evidence to support his theory. He found examples of what had once clearly been molten rocks sitting beside or even inside sedimentary layers. And he found places where sedimentary rocks lay on top of once-molten rocks that had been folded and eroded. There was no way that could have happened in just a few thousand years.

When he presented his ideas in his book *Theory of the Earth* in 1788, few people were convinced. After Hutton's death, however, his friend, the Scottish scientist John Playfair,

wrote a book called *Illustrations of the Huttonian Theory of the Earth* (1802), which explained Hutton's ideas more clearly, and by the 1830s Hutton's insights had become widely accepted.

Hutton had been wondering how big sedimentary rocks could be found above ground, when they had formed under the sea. Then it hit him.

'Hutton's unconformity – newer sedimentary rocks lying on top of older ones that have been tilted upwards

Progress, in tiny bits

Working out that everything really is made of atoms.
Featuring:

Star chemist **Antoine Lavoisier**

Luigi Galvani and his dancing frogs' legs

Alessandro Volta and the first electric battery

Joseph Proust's studies of chemical compounds

John Dalton, who realised that different elements have different weights

John Dalton searching for answers in a glass jar

Lavoisier's landmark chemistry book, *Traité Elémentaire de Chimie (Elementary Treatise of Chemistry)*, 1789.

While James Hutton was busy trying to convince people about his theory of Earth's formation, French chemist Antoine Lavoisier was equally busy, writing the world's first chemistry textbook. The most important idea it contained was that chemical reactions do not create or destroy matter. This idea would lead to an inescapable conclusion: matter really is made of tiny particles.

The big idea in Lavoisier's book is called 'the law of conservation of mass'. The word 'mass' just means 'amount of matter' and you can measure that by weighing. Lavoisier repeatedly weighed everything in his experiments, and he found that in every chemical reaction he observed the total amount of matter (mass) was the same beforehand as it was afterwards – it was conserved. This fitted perfectly with his discovery that chemical reactions are simply the joining or separation of the substances involved – such as when the element hydrogen reacts with the element oxygen to make the compound water – no matter is gained or lost.

In a dramatic confirmation of this idea, in 1800 scientists in England and Germany used a newly invented device, the battery, to successfully split water into its constituent

The electric battery

In the 1780s, Italian scientist Luigi Galvani discovered that electricity could make dead frogs' legs twitch. He carried out many experiments, but in one of them, there seemed to be no electricity involved – Galvani had only to touch the frogs' legs with two different types of metal and they would twitch. Another Italian scientist, Alessandro Volta, surmised that electricity was passing between the two different metals. To prove this, in 1799 he built a pile of copper and zinc discs separated by moist discs of paper. A constant electric current passed between the different metals – Volta had built the world's first battery.

elements, hydrogen and oxygen. Other scientists subsequently used the battery to isolate other elements, notably Humphry Davy, who discovered potassium, sodium, calcium and magnesium in this way.

Gases as elements

The reason why no one had really noticed the conservation of mass before Lavoisier did is that many chemical reactions involve gases. If gases are released into the air during a reaction, the weight of the solid or liquid chemicals decreases; if gases are absorbed from the air during a reaction, the weight of the solid or liquid increases. Lavoisier, however, carried out his reactions in sealed tubes, to prevent gases escaping into the air. To describe the new 'airs', Lavoisier began to use the word 'gas' (*gaz* in French). This helped

Volta's pile: zinc and copper discs separated by discs of moistened card, held in a pile by glass rods

P

n

c

h

z

Dalton's drawings of the atoms of several elements, with estimated atomic weights

ELEMENTS

		wt				wt
⊙	Hydrogen	1	⊕	Strontian	46
⦶	Azote	5	✳	Barytes	68
⬤	Carbon	54	Ⓘ	Iron	50
◯	Oxygen	7	Ⓩ	Zinc	56
⊗	Phosphorus	9	Ⓒ	Copper	56
⊕	Sulphur	13	Ⓛ	Lead	90
◉	Magnesia	20	Ⓢ	Silver	190
⊖	Lime	24	Ⓖ	Gold	190
⦶	Soda	28	Ⓟ	Platina	190
⦶	Potash	42	⊛	Mercury	167

Weighing up the matter

It was left to English chemist John Dalton to make the connection. Dalton was a great believer in the idea that matter is made of tiny particles – atoms. He suggested that each element has different atoms, and when they make a compound, the atoms of one element join to the atoms of another one, in individual clumps that he called 'compound atoms' (today, we call them molecules). So, a compound atom of water, he suggested, would be one atom of hydrogen joined to one atom of oxygen (today, we know that a water molecule is actually made of two atoms of hydrogen and one of oxygen).

Crucially, Dalton realised that atoms of different elements might have different masses. Iron atoms might weigh more than sulphur atoms, for example, and oxygen atoms weigh more than hydrogen atoms. And it turned out that he was right. To see why this was such a breakthrough, imagine joining a 1-kg red ball to a 2-kg blue ball to make a 3-kg 'compound ball'. One hundred of these compound balls would weigh 300 kg, and would be composed of 100 kg of red balls and 200 kg of blue balls. And however many of the compound balls you have, the masses of the red and blue balls will always be in the same proportion. Translate that to atoms and compounds, and this is just what Proust found. All of a sudden, chemical reactions made perfect sense.

In 1808, Dalton published his theory in *A New System of Chemical Philosophy*, and the idea that matter is made of particles became more convincing and more popular than ever.

Every molecule of water (H_2O) is made of three atoms: two of hydrogen, H_2, and one of oxygen, O. Dalton thought it was one H and one O.

scientists think of gases as substances in their own right, just as liquids and solids are.

Lavoisier's discoveries were revolutionary, and they got people thinking. One of them was the French chemist Joseph Proust. Between 1799 and 1803, Proust found that any particular compound is always made of the same proportion of elements by weight. For example, every 100-g sample of tin oxide is made of 88 g of tin and 12 g of oxygen, while every 100-g sample of iron sulphide consists of 64 g of iron and 36 g of sulphur – the masses of the elements in a compound are always in the same proportion. An amazing and quite simple fact was staring Proust in the face, but he missed it.

Making connections

How two forces became one, as established by:

Hans Christian Ørsted, first to notice the effect of electricity on magnetism

André Ampère, who described and measured electromagnetic forces

Joseph Henry and his giant electromagnet

Michael Faraday, creator of the first electric motor

 n 21 April 1820, Danish physics professor Hans Christian Ørsted was giving a private lecture on electricity to a group of his students. During the lecture, Ørsted made a startling discovery. When he connected a wire to each end of a battery, a nearby magnetic compass needle twitched. Ørsted's discovery showed that electricity and magnetism are somehow linked – and it sparked a new effort to 'unify' the forces of nature.

A compass like the one Ørsted used is a magnetised needle that is free to turn and that lines up north–south with Earth's magnetism. As a result, compasses are useful for navigation, and had been employed by Chinese mariners as early as the 11th century.

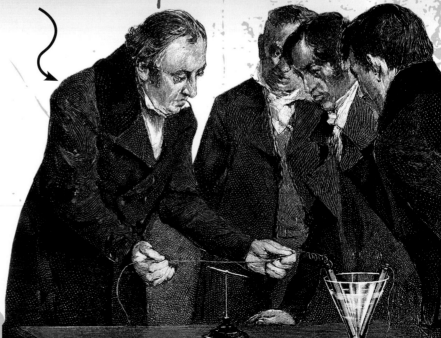

Look, no hands! Ørsted uses an electrical current to make a compass move.

William Gilbert had used compasses in his experiments in the 1590s, and scientists had been using them to investigate magnetism ever since. But they had never used them to experiment with electricity.

Mastering the forces

When Ørsted described his discovery in a pamphlet, the news quickly spread across Europe, and progress in this new field of study was rapid. Within two months, French physicist André Ampère had written a scientific paper on the subject of 'electrodynamics', better known today as electromagnetism.

Ampère realised that Ørsted's compass needle had twitched because the current in the wire was producing a magnetic force. He wondered what would happen if he put two wires near to each other and passed electric current through both. He found that he could make the wires attract or repel, as if they were magnets, and he could control the strength and direction of the force by varying the strength and direction of the electric current in the wires. Ampère went on to discover a precise mathematical law to describe and predict the electromagnetic forces, just as Isaac Newton had done for gravity and motion.

Chinese mariner's compass

A solenoid is just a coil of wire. But send an electric current through it, and it does a good impression of a bar magnet.

Ampère also wound a wire into a coil shape, and found that the magnetic effect was much stronger. He called his coil a 'solenoid', and found that it acted like an ordinary bar-shaped magnet. Ampère's insights also led him to invent the galvanometer, a device that measures the strength of current. The unit of electric current, the amp, is named after him.

Practical applications

Within a year, English physicist and chemist Michael Faraday had harnessed the electromagnetic force to make the world's first electric motor. It consisted of a wire dangling in a dish of mercury, at the centre of which was a magnet. When Faraday connected a battery to the wire and to the mercury, making a complete circuit, a current flowed through the wire and the electromagnetic force caused the wire to move continuously around the magnet. Later, in 1832, English physicist William Sturgeon adapted this principle to make motors that could drive machinery.

In 1824, Sturgeon found that he could make Ampère's solenoid stronger by winding the coil of wire onto an iron rod as its 'core'. Sturgeon had made the first 'electromagnet'. In the late 1820s, US physicist Joseph Henry built a large electromagnet that could lift a 1-tonne weight. Today, electromagnets are found in millions of different devices, from loudspeakers to particle accelerators.

In 1831, Faraday made another startling discovery: not only does electricity make magnetism, but magnetism makes electricity. He discovered that he could produce an electric current in a wire – or better, a coil of wire – whenever he moved it to and fro near a magnet. It didn't matter if he moved the wire or the magnet, the effect was the same. This led to

Joseph Henry's huge electromagnet gave everyone a bit of a lift.

Michael Faraday in his laboratory (below) and (right) some of the coils he wound to experiment with electromagnetism.

the development of the generator, which produces electrical power from motion. Today, generators of one kind or another provide a constant supply of electricity to most homes.

Faraday went on to wrap two coils of wire around a single iron core, and found that he could 'induce' an electric current in one wire by turning a current on and off in the other one. One coil was making magnetism in the iron core, and that magnetism was making electricity in the other coil. This was the forerunner of electric transformers, which play vital roles in modern electricity supplies.

These discoveries in electromagnetism 'unified' the two forces, and put the existence of electric and magnetic fluids in doubt. As a result, scientists began trying to unify all the forces of nature. They wanted to find a simple 'unified' theory that could explain everything. And in the 1840s, they got one.

Mechanical work – or its equivalent as, say, electricity or heat – became known as 'energy'. Things that had the potential to do work – like Joule's weights before he let them fall – were said to have 'potential energy'. Joule had shown that it was possible to trace energy as it changes from one form to another; in turn, the idea of energy linked the various forces of nature in one unified concept.

It was also clear that energy, like mass, must be 'conserved'. You can't create energy, nor can you destroy it: energy just changes from one form to another, and there is a fixed amount of it in the Universe. These were profound ideas.

Thermodynamics and particles

In the 1850s, the idea that energy is conserved became the first 'law' of a new branch of science called thermodynamics. A central idea in thermodynamics is that temperature is directly related to the motion of the tiny particles of which matter is made. The faster an object's particles move (on average), the higher is its temperature. Heat is the transfer of energy to an object's particles. So, transferring heat to a flask of water increases the speed at which the water's particles move – and its temperature rises.

Once the water reaches boiling point, however, any extra heat you add is directed into breaking the forces that hold the molecules of water together as a liquid and releasing them as a gas. This idea made scientists realise that gases were also made of particles flying around at high speed – just as Daniel Bernoulli had suggested more than 100 years earlier.

Heat is a form of energy: it can 'do work'. When water boils, the heat does work on the water molecules, breaking them apart to make a vapour.

James Joule, with his paddle wheel. Below: the paddle wheel, in action, driven by the energy of falling weights

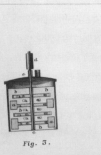

Fig. 2.

Fig. 3.

The evolution of an idea *

Revealing how species come and go, with:

Carolus Linnaeus, who created a classification system for plants and animals

Charles Darwin and his theory of natural selection

T he concept of energy was to become one of the most fundamental ideas in science. And soon after, in the 1860s, another enormously important idea rocked the world of science – this time in biology, the study of living things. Formulated by English naturalist Charles Darwin, it was the theory of evolution by natural selection.

Darwin's theory provided a powerful explanation of how species of plants and animals develop – or evolve – over long periods of time. This was an idea that had occurred to some earlier scientists. But it was one that was very much at odds with contemporary beliefs, which were based on the biblical view of nature: that God had created the world, and plants and animals, and that since then they hadn't changed one bit.

Biologists of the 1700s, such as Linnaeus (right), could classify plants and animals, but had little hope of understanding them.

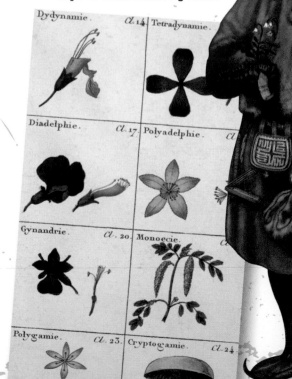

Dydynamie. *Cl.* 14 Tetradynamie.

Diadelphie. *Cl.* 17 Polyadelphie. *Cl.*

Gynandrie. *Cl.* 20. Monoecie. *Cl.*

Polygamie. *Cl.* 23. Cryptogamie. *Cl.* 24

Finding order in nature

Biology had been a little slow to benefit from the scientific method. The main reason for this was that living things seemed so much more complex than non-living matter. The growth and movements of plants and animals could not be predicted with Newton's laws of motion; and scientific experiments could do little to make sense of how living things worked. Anatomists had cut up and studied bodies but had little idea of what was going on inside them. As a result, medicine was based mainly on superstition, guesswork and alchemy, not hard science.

In the 18th century, however, scientists began to study plants (botany) and animals (zoology) more systematically. In the 1750s, Danish botanist Carolus Linnaeus made some sense of the enormous diversity of nature, with a system of classification that allowed scientists working in any language to refer to the same species using its Latin name. And in the middle of the 19th century, improvements in microscopes, the understanding of chemistry and communications between scientists helped the scientific study of biology pick up pace.

Incremental changes

Soon after he finished university in 1831, Charles Darwin sailed around the world as a naturalist on a scientific expedition, aboard the HMS *Beagle*. During his voyage, Darwin read a book by Scottish geologist Charles Lyell, which explained James Hutton's theory about how the landscape had formed over millions of years. As he travelled, Darwin saw plenty of evidence to back up Hutton's theory. For example, in Chile,

he experienced an earthquake during which the land shifted by several metres.

While collecting and classifying plants and animals during what turned out to be a five-year journey, Darwin was struck by how well different species were adapted to their environments. Once home, he began to make connections between the adaptations he had seen around the world and the way farmers and animal breeders in England could

change the characteristics of plants and animals. Pigeon breeders, for example, could produce birds with a variety of different colours, shapes and sizes by careful 'selection' of particular birds to mate.

Darwin realised that species in the wild change, too, by 'natural selection'. He reasoned that small random changes – mutations – must happen when a plant or animal reproduces, and that these mutations change the characteristics of the offspring slightly. Mutations that improve the chances of survival are carried to the next generation. This idea explains why plants and animals are so well adapted to their environments: as an environment changes, or an organism moves to a different environment, any mutations that make an organism better suited to that environment are more likely to

HMS *Beagle* anchored off the coast of South America.

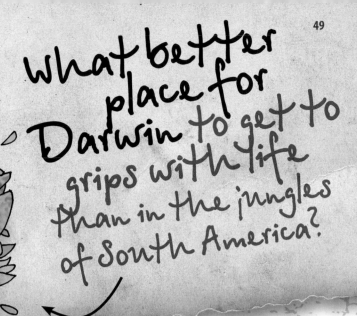

A controversial theory

During the 1840s and 1850s, Darwin carried out hundreds of experiments, mostly on plants in his garden. Although he couldn't watch species evolve over millions of years, he did find plenty of evidence to support his theory – and little to contradict it.

Darwin's theory was revolutionary but so well backed up by observation and experiments that it was irresistible. Linnaeus's system of classification had encouraged naturalists to think about how animals and plants are related to each other; anatomy had demonstrated the similarities between different animals; fossils had revealed plant and animal species that no longer existed. Darwin's theory made sense of it all.

Darwin set out his ideas in a book called *On the Origin of Species by Means of Natural Selection*, published in 1859. He knew it would be controversial, particularly among religious people, and it was. One criticism of Darwin's theory was that he could not suggest a mechanism through which mutation could happen – something of which he was well aware. It would be another 50 years before scientists began working out that mechanism, and how characteristics are inherited from generation to generation.

Darwin made sense of evolution by thinking of new species as new branches of an ever-growing tree.

be passed down. Over long periods of time, the small mutations result in entirely new species.

In 1836, Darwin concluded that if his theory were correct, then some species would die out altogether, some would change and others would split into two different species. He began to see that all living things are part of the same family tree. Look back far enough in time, and you would see that, say, all fish come from a single ancestor that lived millions of years ago; the same would be true for mammals, reptiles, birds, insects and plants. Look back even further, and you would see that every living thing may have come from a single species.

Light
relief

Probing the true nature of light, as revealed by:

Thomas Young and the wave theory

Hippolyte Fizeau, calculator of the speed of light

Michael Faraday, who linked light with magnetism

James Clerk Maxwell, who found an answer in numbers

A few years after Darwin published his theory of evolution, Scottish physicist James Clerk Maxwell made a momentous discovery about the nature of light. And to everyone's surprise, it turned out that light had a lot to do with electricity and magnetism.

Scientists had long debated the nature of light. Isaac Newton, for example, believed that light was a stream of particles, while 17th-century Dutch physicist Christiaan Huygens suggested that light behaved more like waves or ripples on the surface of a pond. In the 19th century, the wave theory became more popular after English physicist Thomas Young carried out a series of experiments that showed water waves behaving just like light.

Across the spectrum

Newton had shown that white light is made of a spectrum of colours, across which the colours run from red, at one end, through yellow and green to violet, at the other end. According to the wave theory, each colour in the spectrum corresponds to a different frequency of vibration – how rapidly the wave waves. This is similar to the way in which the frequency of a sound wave determines its pitch – how high or low it sounds.

Ripples in water behave just like light waves.

The colours in sunlight make up the 'visible' spectrum. Beyond the red end is infrared radiation; beyond the violet end is ultraviolet radiation.

And so, in 1800, when astronomer William Herschel noticed that a thermometer placed just beyond the red end of the spectrum would register a slight rise in temperature and suggested it might be due to an invisible form of light, scientists surmised that this invisible light had a lower frequency than red light. Today we call it infrared radiation. A year later, inspired by Herschel, German physicist Johann Ritter used light-sensitive chemicals to detect invisible light beyond the blue end of the spectrum – light which, it followed, had a higher frequency than blue light. Today we call that invisible light 'ultraviolet radiation'.

The speed of light

Whatever the nature of light – either waves or particles – one thing scientists could at least try to measure was its speed. It had long been clear that light travels very fast – some people thought it might have infinite speed. The first realistic estimates of the speed of light were made in the 18th century, from astronomical observations. And in 1849, French physicist Hippolyte Fizeau conducted the first accurate ground-based measurements

Fizeau set up a source of light behind a rapidly rotating toothed wheel and placed a mirror 8 km away, in line with the light. The light passed through the gaps in the edge of the wheel and was chopped up into pulses by the wheel's teeth. The pulses bounced off the mirror and back to the apparatus, a journey that took just a tiny fraction of a second. At a certain speed of rotation, a light

Fizeau had finally seen – and measured – the light. His assistant had blinked and missed it.

pulse would be arriving back at the wheel just as the next gap between the teeth was moving into place – only then could Fizeau see the returning light. Based on the speed of the wheel and the distance between the teeth, Fizeau could work out how fast the light must have been travelling. He came up with a result that was pretty close to the actual figure, which is just under 300,000 km per second.

Faraday coined the word 'field' to describe the area affected by magnets and electric charges, and mapped out invisible lines of force.

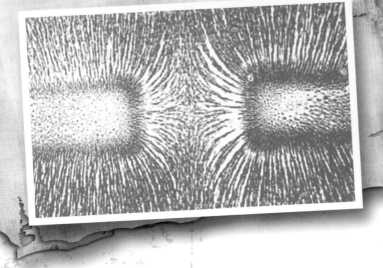

combined electric and magnetic fields that propagate each other – one electric field creates a magnetic field that creates an electric field, and so on. This happens almost instantly, causing light to travel at tremendous speed.

Off the scale

The equations revealed more: they suggested there might be other forms of electromagnetic radiation, with frequencies even lower than infrared and higher than ultraviolet. In 1887, German physicist Heinrich Hertz discovered low-frequency radiation: radio waves. Within another 15 years, scientists found two types of high-frequency radiation: X-rays (1895) and gamma rays (1900). Thus it was shown that all forms of electromagnetic radiation are identical – apart from their frequency.

Light and magnetism

In 1845, Michael Faraday conducted a complex experiment that demonstrated that light was affected by magnetism. The forces of nature were becoming more unified, but scientists had no idea how magnetism could affect light. In the same year, Faraday coined the term 'field' to describe the area of force around magnets and electrically charged objects. Faraday was a brilliant practical scientist, but not a mathematician, so he was unable to work out equations to describe and predict electric and magnetic fields and how they interact. That challenge was taken up by Scottish physicist James Clerk Maxwell.

In 1861, Maxwell condensed everything that was known about the interaction of electricity and magnetism into four 'field equations'. Even more remarkably, in 1864 he combined his four equations into just one – and he recognised at once what type of equation he was left with. It was the type of equation that describes waves. And when he worked out the speed of the waves his equation described, it matched exactly the speed of light. Maxwell had shown that all forms of light consist of

Electric Field

Magnetic Field

Direction of travel

A representation of an electromagnetic wave, with the electric and magnetic fields at right angles to each other.

'The direction of the electric displacement is at the right angles to the magnetic disturbance, and both at right angles to the direction of the ray.'

JAMES MAXWELL, 1864

An elementary system

Revealing hidden patterns in chemistry, as identified by:

Gustav Kirchhoff and **Robert Bunsen**, inventors of spectroscopy

John Newlands, who noted repeating sequences of elements

Dmitri Mendeleev, creator of the periodic table

T he new theories about energy, evolution and electromagnetic radiation were impressive leaps forward. And soon it was clear that deep truths lay undiscovered in chemistry, too – and Russian chemist Dmitri Mendeleev was keen to find them.

By the mid-1800s, chemistry had come a long way since Lavoisier had discovered the basic facts about elements, compounds and chemical reactions in the 1780s. An exciting development was the discovery of numerous previously undiscovered chemical elements. In 1789, Lavoisier knew of 23 elements; by the end of the 1850s, the list had grown to 58. And in 1860, two German physicists, Gustav Kirchoff and Robert Bunsen, using a device called a spectroscope, found the 59th.

Bunsen and Kirchhoff's spectroscope shed new light on chemistry.

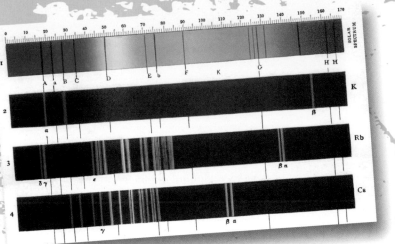

SOLAR SPECTRUM

Reading the lines

Kirchoff and Bunsen had realised that if they heated a sample of an element and passed it through a prism, it produced a pattern, or spectrum, of coloured bars, and that each element produced a different pattern. So they built a device for doing this – the spectroscope. And when they then discovered a pattern of colours they did not recognise, they knew they had found a new element,

The spectra of sunlight (top) and the elements potassium (K), rubidium (Rb) and caesium (Cs), from Bunsen and Kirchhoff's drawings.

now called caesium. Soon after, in 1868, French astronomer Pierre Janssen passed sunlight through a prism, and noticed a previously unknown line in its spectrum. He had discovered another new element, later named helium, after the Greek word for the Sun, *helios*.

Seeking connections

By 1870, chemists had identified 63 elements, and they started studying connections between them that might reveal an underlying pattern. They noticed, for example, that carbon and silicon were both non-metals that formed similar compounds, and that lithium and sodium were both soft, reactive metals.

John Dalton had worked out that atoms of different elements had different weights, and since then, chemists had made accurate measurements of the atomic weights for all the known elements. In 1865, English chemist John Newlands arranged the elements in ascending order of atomic weights, and

All of a kind

Friedrich Wöhler

Another major achievement of early 19th-century chemistry was to show that chemical reactions in living things were no different from those in the laboratory. Living things are made almost entirely of compounds of the element carbon: so-called organic compounds. Scientists and philosophers had long believed that organic substances were different from other, 'inorganic' ones – that they possessed some sort of vital force or living spirit. But in 1828, German chemist Friedrich Wöhler overturned that idea when he made the organic compound urea from inorganic ingredients.

Normally clear crystals of the organic compound urea, photographed through polaroid filters.

element and its atomic weight, and laid them out on a table in various ways. When he arranged them into several rows, or 'periods', of eight, then eight again, then eighteen, starting at top left and running in order of atomic weight, he found that the columns represented 'groups' of elements with similar properties. A pattern was taking shape.

Though there were gaps in his 'periodic table', Mendeleev realised that they simply represented elements that had yet to be discovered and he even closely predicted the properties and atomic weights of three of the missing elements, which were discovered in the next few years. Today, 118 elements are known. And although the exact layout of the periodic table has had to be modified slightly, Mendeleev's basic structure of groups and periods remains accurate.

The periodic table illustrates the order in the structure of atoms. It is like a handy map of the landscape of chemistry, and it was to prove a very useful guide to scientists in the years to come as they began to uncover the secrets of the world inside the atom.

Even playing without a full deck, Mendeleev managed to find order in chemistry.

found the beginnings of a pattern. Newlands noticed that every eight elements along the sequence, chemical properties seemed to repeat – they were 'periodic'. Lithium and sodium were in positions 2 and 10, for example, and carbon and silicon were numbers 5 and 13. But Newlands' pattern only worked for the first twenty or so elements, and he was ridiculed for even suggesting that it might be significant. This was a shame, because he was onto something.

Cards on the table

Dmitri Mendeleev had also noticed that elements' properties were periodic. In 1869, he made cards, each bearing the name of an

The periodic table, with its periods (rows) and groups (columns)

Wash your hands

In the 19th century, surgeons performed operations using kits like this.

Finding out about germs, in the company of:

Ignaz Semmelweis, pioneer hygienist

Louis Pasteur, who worked out why things 'go bad'

Joseph Lister and his antiseptic spray

Robert Koch, who identified the culprits causing tuberculosis and cholera

The second half of the 19th century was a time of rapid change, particularly in Europe and North America. People had access to new technologies, but many moved into cities, where health was poor and they often died young from diseases that are easily cured today.

Progress in physics and chemistry played a key role in many of the new technologies of the time. For example, the telegraph, which allowed instant long-distance communication, depended upon electromagnetism. Synthetic chemicals (ones not found in nature), such as colourful dyes, were manufactured in plentiful supply in the factories of the rapidly growing chemical industry.

Biology, however, played less of a role in the dramatic changes taking place in society. Botanists and zoologists still had little idea of how plants and animals actually work, and the new theory of evolution had no practical applications. In medicine, doctors had learned enough about the inside of the human body to carry out quite complicated surgery. But many patients died soon after operations, and people continued to die even from simple cuts and grazes. And no one knew why.

Hospital hygiene

In 1847, Hungarian doctor Ignaz Semmelweis made an amazing discovery that appears obvious to us today: washing your hands can prevent the spread of disease. Semmelweis was working in a hospital where about one in ten women died soon after childbirth, usually from a form of sepsis, or 'blood poisoning', called childbed fever. In another, nearby hospital, however, the death rate was less than one in twenty.

Semmelweis compared the conditions in the two hospitals and realised that doctors in his hospital often attended to women giving birth after they had carried out post-mortem examinations (on dead bodies). He realised that something from the dead bodies was sticking to the doctors' hands and causing the women to become ill. Simply by getting the doctors to wash their hands after touching the dead bodies, Semmelweis was able to reduce the death rate among women in childbirth by 90 per cent.

Miasma or bacteria?

Unfortunately, few people took much notice of Semmelweis's results. At the time, most scientists didn't think that disease spread from person to person but originated in materials like rotting vegetables or sewage in open sewers and then spread as foul-smelling air, referred to as 'miasma'. So they couldn't see how washing your hands would help. This miasma theory did at least lead to some cities having enclosed sewage systems and laws to limit the spread of foul airs. But diseases such as cholera and diphtheria, as well as infected wounds, still claimed millions of lives.

In the 1850s, some scientists suggested that the real cause of diseases might be

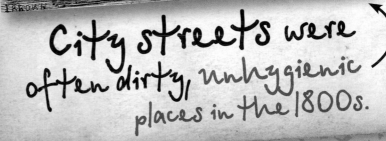

City streets were often dirty, unhygienic places in the 1800s.

Ignaz Semmelweis worked out a simple way to limit the spread of disease.

microorganisms – tiny living things that could only be seen under a microscope. These were the 'animalcules' that Leeuwenhoek had first seen 200 years earlier. Disease-carrying microorganisms were sometimes referred to as 'germs', so this alternative to the miasma theory became known as the 'germ theory'.

Germs are in fact single-celled organisms more correctly called bacteria (singular: bacterium). Scientists were by this time beginning to understand that all living things are made of cells. Furthermore, in the 1840s Polish scientist Robert Remak had shown that cells could only be created from other cells. Until then, scientists had believed that living things could come from non-living things – an idea called 'spontaneous generation'.

In a brilliant experiment, French microbiologist Louis Pasteur proved that Remak's idea was correct. Pasteur made some broth and boiled it in a flask with a bent spout. Normally, broth would turn cloudy after a day or two and go bad. But the boiling killed any bacteria that were in the broth; furthermore, the bent spout prevented any bacteria from reaching the broth from the air. As a result, the broth remained clear and fresh for much longer than normal. It only started spoiling again after it was left open to the air, when airborne bacteria could land in it and start reproducing. Pasteur's work gave support to the germ theory, and it even showed how

Cell theory

When German scientists Theodor Schwann and Matthias Schleiden met in 1838, they developed the theory that the cell is the basic unit of all living things. Previously, Schwann had realised that animals are made of cells, while Schleiden had realised the same thing about plants. Even bacteria are made of cells – but in their case, just one.

Human skin cells seen through a microscope. Each cell has a nucleus – the dark blobs.

Louis Pasteur peering through a microscope and trying to work out if he has bad broth

Joseph Lister got quite carried away with his new carbolic acid spray.

germs could be easily killed, using heat – he went on to suggest that bacteria could also be killed by certain chemicals.

Prevention and cure

Scottish surgeon Joseph Lister was inspired by Pasteur's experiment. In 1865, Lister began using a solution of carbolic acid (now known as phenol) to kill bacteria in situations where the body was open and vulnerable to infection. Initially, he soaked bandages in the solution, and wrapped them around open wounds. Then he started washing his hands and cleaning his surgical instruments in the carbolic acid, too, and designed a device that would spray a fine mist of it around his operating theatre. The rate of infection and death in his hospital plummeted.

In 1876, German doctor and microbiologist Robert Koch managed to identify the species of bacterium that causes a deadly disease called anthrax – the first time a specific bacterium had been linked to a particular disease. He went on to identify the bacteria that cause cholera and tuberculosis. In the 1880s, Pasteur and his assistants developed

Vaccines like this one can prevent bacterial and viral diseases, by encouraging the body to prepare a defence.

vaccines that made chickens immune to cholera and sheep immune to anthrax. A vaccine is a weak form of a disease injected into the body, which causes the immune system to produce proteins called antibodies that fight the disease. No one understood why vaccines were successful until the discovery of how antibodies work, in the 1930s.

As another means of purifying liquids, Pasteur and his team also developed a porcelain filter, with tiny perforations. When a liquid was poured through the filter, any bacteria in it would be trapped, leaving the solution sterile. In 1887, Russian microbiologist Dmitry Ivanovsky was using a filter of this type to investigate a disease in tobacco plants. When the filter failed to make his solutions sterile, Ivanovsky realised that the disease was being caused by something much smaller than bacteria. In 1898, Dutch microbiologist Martinus Beijerinck named that something a 'virus'.

These discoveries of bacteria and viruses as disease-causing 'pathogens' soon helped improve public health and prevent millions of deaths, and would also lead to breakthroughs in medicine in the 20th century.

Episode 17

Smaller than atoms

Exploring a new world of tiny particles, as unveiled by:

JJ Thomson, discoverer of the electron

Marie Curie, who isolated radioactive elements

Ernest Rutherford, who painted a picture of atomic structure

JJ Thomson, the first person to discover something smaller than an atom.

While Pasteur and Koch were looking at tiny micro-organisms through their microscopes, an English physicist named JJ Thomson was investigating even tinier things – smaller even than atoms.

Until the 1890s, scientists believed that atoms were solid balls – the 'uncuttable' smallest parts of matter. In 1897, however, Thomson discovered the electron, an even smaller particle, and thus began a voyage of discovery inside the atom.

Found in every atom, electrons are particles that carry negative electric charge. Every atom contains positive electric charge, too, and overall the charges in an atom balance. But electrons are tiny, and they can be separated from atoms. And that simple fact was the cause of many phenomena that had puzzled scientists for more than 100 years, including static electricity, electric current and chemical reactions.

Thomson discovered the electron using a cathode ray tube: a sealed glass tube from which most of the air has been removed. Inside the tube are two metal electrodes connected to an electricity supply. Electric current flows between the electrodes as an invisible 'ray' that passes through the vacuum. Thomson noted that the ray always flowed from the negative electrode (known as the cathode) towards the positive electrode (anode), which indicated that it must be negatively charged. He then showed that the

What are these particles?

Are they atoms, or molecules, or matter in a still finer state of subdivision?' JJ THOMSON, 1895

Thomson's cathode ray tube. Rays from the circular cathode (right) shot past the anode (the dark band at the start of the straight tube) and were deflected by an electric field between the two plates in the middle.

ray was actually a beam of particles, and he found that those particles were much lighter than the lightest type of atom, hydrogen.

Mysterious rays

In 1898, Polish scientist Marie Curie began uncovering another secret of the world inside the atom, while exploring the strange behaviour of compounds of the element uranium. Curie had been investigating French physicist Henri Becquerel's 1896 discovery that an ore containing the element uranium emitted invisible rays. Curie worked out that the rays were coming from within the atoms of uranium, and she named this phenomenon 'radioactivity', from *radius*, the Latin word for ray.

Assisted by her husband Pierre, Curie then experimented with all the known elements to see if any others were radioactive. She found one that was, thorium, and another two previously undiscovered substances that were also radioactive, polonium and radium. To prove these were new elements, she had to extract samples from uranium ore, by boiling, filtering and purifying. After three years of hard work, the Curies had extracted just a few grams of radium from several tonnes of ore.

Atomic structure

In 1899, New Zealand-born physicist Ernest Rutherford found that there were two types of ray produced by radioactive substances, which

Nearly done! In three years of hot, heavy toil, the Curies worked through several tonnes of uranium ore.

Nobel Prize

Every year since 1901, an organisation called the Nobel Foundation, set up by the wealthy Swedish inventor of dynamite, Alfred Nobel, has awarded lucrative prizes for the most outstanding work carried out in the fields of physics, chemistry, physiology or medicine, literature and international relations. Several of the scientists who helped to discover the inner structure of the atom won a Nobel prize, including Henri Becquerel (1903), Marie Curie (1903 and 1911), Pierre Curie (1903), JJ Thomson (1906), Ernest Rutherford (1908) and James Chadwick (1935).

Nobel Prize medal awarded to JJ Thomson in 1906.

'It was almost as if you fired a 15-inch shell at a piece of tissue paper and it came back and hit you.'

ERNEST RUTHERFORD (ABOVE) ON THE GOLD-FOIL EXPERIMENT

he named 'alpha' and 'beta' rays, after the first two letters of the Greek alphabet. Rutherford found that these rays were streams of tiny, electrically charged particles: fragments of atoms breaking up or 'disintegrating'. In 1900, French physicist Paul Villard discovered that radioactive substances produce a third type of ray, which he called 'gamma' (the third letter of the Greek alphabet). Villard found that gamma rays are a form of electromagnetic radiation – like light, X-rays and radio waves.

To work out the structure of the atom, in 1911 two of Rutherford's students fired alpha particles at a thin gold-foil. Most of the alpha particles passed almost straight through the foil, but some bounced back. This suggested to Rutherford that an atom most likely consisted of a tiny, positively charged, very dense core (which he called the nucleus), around which minuscule, negatively charged electrons orbited in a larger space – rather like planets orbiting the Sun. In the gold-foil experiment, most of the positively charged alpha particles were able to pass

Rutherford's idea of what an atom might be like: electrons orbit a heavy, positively charged nucleus.

through the spaces between nuclei. But a few, intriguingly, collided with and were repelled by the nucleus's concentrated positive charge.

In 1918, Rutherford found that the nucleus was not just a single blob of positive charge: it contained positively charged particles, which he called protons. Each proton carries the same amount of charge as each electron, only positive rather than negative, and the number of protons in the nucleus determines which element a particular atom is. Hydrogen has one proton, while oxygen has eight, for example.

Because all the protons are positively charged, they repel each other, making a nucleus unstable. A large nucleus would be more unstable than a small one, which explains why uranium, with 92 protons, and radium, with 88, are radioactive. In 1932, English physicist James Chadwick showed that the nucleus contains another type of particle with no electric charge, the neutron.

Relatively revolutionary

Adventures in time and space, starring:

Albert Einstein, who realised everything in space is relative

Hermann Minkowski and the fourth dimension

Arthur Eddington, who demonstrated Einstein's theories in action

Albert Einstein photographed in 1920, five years after the publication of his second theory of relativity.

Eight years after JJ Thompson discovered the electron, a German physicist called Albert Einstein published the first of his two theories of 'relativity', which revolutionised our understanding of space, time, motion and gravity.

In 1869, James Clerk Maxwell had suggested that it might be possible for scientists to determine Earth's actual, or 'absolute', speed through space. Until then, they could only measure our planet's speed relative to the Sun and the other planets – which are also moving through space. This is like a sailor only being able to work out his or her boat's speed relative to other moving boats, rather than its absolute speed through the water.

The equations that Maxwell had worked out in the 1860s suggested that light was an electromagnetic wave travelling through space at a particular speed. Scientists expected that if they measured the speed of light, it would vary depending on whether they were travelling towards it or away from it. For example, it made sense that if you were moving at speed and shone a torch in the direction of travel, you would 'catch up' with the light waves slightly and measure their speed as slightly lower; indeed, if you travelled at the speed of light, you would keep up with the waves, and their speed would be zero. Conversely, if you shone your torch in the opposite direction, you would 'leave the waves behind', and measure their speed as slightly higher.

Puzzling result

During the 1870s and 1880s several scientists tried to detect the difference in speed between beams of light travelling in different directions in space. But however they tried, they found nothing: the speed of light was always exactly the same. Throughout the 1890s, scientists realised that the only way they could explain this strange result was if they accepted that measurements of distance always depend upon your motion through space. They also suggested that time might run at different rates – that there might be a 'universal time' for empty space and a 'local time' for objects moving through it.

In 1905, in his scientific paper *On the Electrodynamics of Moving Bodies*, Albert Einstein showed that these strange ideas were not far from the truth. Distance and time really are 'relative'. He also showed that there is no 'universal time' and no 'absolute rest'. Scientists travelling relative to each other will measure times and distances differently. The effect is only noticeable at very high relative speeds – close to the speed of light – which is why no one had ever noticed it before.

Relative time

To understand these basic ideas of Einstein's theory, imagine a spaceship, in which an astronaut shines a torch at a mirror in the ceiling. From the point of view of the astronaut or anyone else in the spaceship,

Viewed from outside, a light shone on a mirror inside a passing spaceship will appear to take longer to reach the mirror, and cover a greater distance.

According to the General Theory of Relativity, gravity is caused by the bending of space-time around objects with mass.

the torchlight follows a short path straight up to the mirror and back. Now imagine you are in another spaceship, whizzing past the first one in the opposite direction. From your point of view, or 'frame of reference', the torchlight follows a longer, diagonal path. Since the speed of light is always the same, it must be that the light takes longer to reach the mirror *in your frame of reference* than it does in the other astronaut's frame of reference. The same two events – light leaving the torch and arriving at the mirror – are separated by different amounts of time, depending on whether you are at rest relative to the mirror (inside the first spaceship) or moving relative to the mirror (watching that spaceship whizz past).

Mass and energy

As part of his theory of relativity Einstein worked out equations that showed that an object's mass is really just a measure of its total energy. As an object increases in speed, it gains energy, and its mass increases. The equations showed that when an object stops moving, it still has energy.

The complicated mathematics reduced to a handy equation – one that became the most famous in science: $E = mc^2$. In the equation, 'E' stands for energy, 'm' stands for mass and 'c^2' is 'c-squared', the speed of light (c) multiplied by itself. Einstein had shown that it is not mass or energy that is conserved, but a new quantity: 'mass-energy'.

'Space by itself and time by itself, are doomed to fade away into mere shadows, and only a kind of union of the two will preserve an independent reality.' HERMANN MINKOWSKI, 1908

Gravity, space and time

Attempts to make sense of Einstein's theory of relativity led German mathematician Hermann Minkowski to consider time as a 'fourth dimension' in the Universe. His idea of four-dimensional 'space-time' helped physicists to picture and work out the consequences of relativity.

In 1915, Einstein published a second theory of relativity – he now called his first one 'Special' and his second 'General'. The General Theory of Relativity explained gravity and showed how it, too, affects time and space. According to the theory, gravity can be understood as the 'bending' of space-time around massive objects.

Eddington's photo of the 1919 solar eclipse. You can make out some stars around the blocked-out Sun.

With his thoughts taken up by relativity, Einstein would frequently lose track of time.

Time differences

Einstein's theories also meant that some really strange things could occur, though only at extremes of speed or gravity – you would seldom be able to see them happening. For example, a clock at the bottom of a very tall building will run fractionally slower than one at the top of the building. Also, in a vehicle travelling close to the speed of light, time will run more slowly than it does at rest. So one person could travel in a spaceship at that speed for some time and return to Earth to find that much more time has passed there.

Proved right

Using mathematical equations, Einstein could carry out experiments that he could never have conducted in the real world. Amazingly, the findings of his mathematical 'thought experiments' have since been proved correct in the real world, time and time again – most famously, during a total solar eclipse in 1919.

A total solar eclipse happens when the Moon completely covers the Sun, as seen from Earth; as a result, the normally bright daytime sky becomes dark enough to see the stars. English astronomer Arthur Eddington used the 1919 eclipse to compare Einstein's General Theory with Isaac Newton's law of gravitation. Both theories suggested that light is deflected when it passes near a massive object, but they differed on the degree of deflection. Eddington took photographs of the stars in the sky near to the blocked-out Sun that showed that their positions had shifted from where they would normally be – as anticipated, the huge mass of the Sun had deflected their light. The shift in the positions of the stars was exactly as Einstein's theory had predicted, not Newton's.

News of Einstein's triumph spread quickly around the world – and beyond the world of science. From then on, he became an international celebrity and his name was forever linked to the idea of genius.

Pass it On

Solving the mysteries of inheritance, thanks to:

Gregor Mendel and his pea plants

Walther Flemming, discoverer of chromosomes

Walter Sutton, who saw that chromosomes carry genes

Thomas Hunt Morgan and his cast of thousands of fruit flies

By the early 20th century, nearly all scientists accepted Charles Darwin's theory of evolution. However, Darwin's theory begged the question of 'inheritance': how could characteristics be transferred from one generation of living things to the next?

Even as Darwin was making his theory public, in 1859 an Austrian friar named Gregor Mendel was working out the 'laws' of inheritance in a remarkable series of experiments with peas. In 1856, Mendel set out to produce a 'hybrid' of pea plant varieties that would combine the best qualities of each. In eight years, he grew more than 10,000 pea plants, crossbreeding them and noting how different characteristics, or traits, were passed on.

Hidden traits

Mendel focused on seven simple traits, each with just two possible versions; for example, the *colour* of the peas (one trait) could be yellow or green. A simple rule emerged from his experiments: one form of each trait seemed 'dominant', and occurred in an average of three out of four offspring; the other was 'recessive', appearing in one out of every four. Nature, it seemed, was throwing loaded dice.

Gregor Mendel wonders how alike two peas in a pod really are.

Mendel worked out that pea colour is determined by particles he called 'elements'. Each plant receives two elements: one from each parent. Furthermore, the element comes in two versions: green (g) and yellow (y). As a result, a plant will receive one of four combinations of elements: gg, gy, yg and yy. If two elements are the same (gg or yy), the plant will be that colour. But if there is one of each (gy or yg), the dominant trait – in this case the yellow – will prevail. That explained why three out of four plants had yellow peas. Moreover, Mendel realised that *every* trait, not just pea colour, must be determined by elements in this way. Some elements would have several versions, and most traits would be determined by more than one element.

Mendel's ideas explained how some characteristics could disappear in one generation, only to reappear again in later ones – traits can be 'carried' down the line, but, if they are recessive, they can remain hidden or 'unexpressed' for generations. In 1865, Mendel presented his discoveries to his local Society of Natural Science, and afterwards, he wrote up his results, and sent copies to two well-known professors of botany. But no one took any notice.

Walther Flemming's sketches of chromosomes in cell nuclei

One generation of crossing a yellow with a green pea plant. On average, three out of four of the offspring will be yellow, since the yellow element is dominant.

Combining chromosomes

Meanwhile, biologists were busy peering down their microscopes into plant and animal cells and had become particularly interested in the nucleus, a dark area found inside nearly every type of cell. In 1878, German biologist Walther Flemming discovered tiny structures inside the nucleus – structures we now call 'chromosomes'. Flemming saw these structures become long and stringy during cell division (when one cell becomes two) and he saw the chromosomes shared out between the 'parent' and 'offspring' cells. But since he knew nothing of Mendel's experiments, he didn't make any connection between chromosomes and inheritance.

In 1898, German biologist Theodor Boveri realised that egg and sperm cells in animals and pollen cells and ovules in plants had only half as many chromosomes as other cells. When fertilisation takes place – when an egg and a sperm or a pollen cell and an ovule join – the full number of chromosomes is present once again. In 1902, American biologist Walter

Sutton made the connection between this process and Mendel's laws of inheritance, which had been rediscovered in 1900, 16 years after Mendel's death. Sutton realised that the chromosomes must somehow carry Mendel's elements. In 1905, English biologist William Bateson suggested that the study of inheritance should be called 'genetics'. Four years later, Danish botanist Wilhelm Johannsen coined the word 'gene' for Mendel's elements.

The association of paternal and maternal chromosomes in pairs...may constitute the physical basis of the Mendelian law of heredity.' WALTER SUTTON, 1902

On the fly

Proof of Sutton's idea – that genes are carried on chromosomes – came from an unusual laboratory in the university where Sutton had worked. In 1910, US biologist

Thomas Hunt Morgan at his microscope. His diagrams (right) show how a parent's chromosomes can mix up genes along their length, creating a new, unique chromosome inside an egg or sperm.

Thomas Hunt Morgan set up 'The Fly Room', filled with hundreds of bottles containing fruit flies. Morgan chose fruit flies for his experiments because they have a very short life cycle, need very little food and are small enough to be kept in vast numbers. They have since become one of the standard organisms used to investigate genetics.

Gazing through microscopes and carefully crossing flies with various traits, Morgan and his team managed to map out which traits are carried on which chromosomes. In 1926, one of Morgan's colleagues, Hermann Müller, managed to produce fruit flies with mutations – mistakes in the copying of information in genes – by irradiating the flies with X-rays.

Mistakes that work

In 1930, in a book called *The Genetical Theory of Natural Selection*, Morgan explained the role of genes and chromosomes in evolution. Genes, carried on chromosomes inside the cell nucleus, pass information from generation to generation. The mutations necessary for evolution to happen are 'mistakes' in copying information in genes, like the ones Müller had produced. Some mutations produce new traits that give an individual some kind of advantage over its kin. Those individuals are more likely to survive, so the mutation becomes established. Eventually, after an accumulation of mutations, a new species may arise.

One important question still remained: how could chromosomes carry information? The answer to that would come in the 1950s, when scientists discovered the structure of a chemical compound called DNA.

How big is the Universe?

Peering into deep, deep space, along with:

Friedrich Bessel and the parallax technique

Henrietta Leavitt and her comparisons of variable stars

Edwin Hubble, who realised the Universe is forever getting bigger

By the beginning of the 20th century, scientists' understanding of outer space had come a long way since the days of Kepler, Galileo and Newton. But there were still some basic questions to be answered. For example: How big is the Universe?

In April 1920, US astronomers Harlow Shapley and Heber Curtis held a public debate about the size of the Universe. All the stars we can see in the night sky are part of a group called the Milky Way galaxy. But scientists had found hundreds of other, fuzzy objects in space, which they called 'nebulas'. Curtis argued that these were other galaxies. Shapley and most other astronomers, on the other hand, believed that there couldn't be anything

Heber Curtis, who argued in favour of Andromeda and other nebulas being 'island universes' – galaxies outside our own.

beyond the Milky Way – partly because the distances involved would be unthinkably enormous. The arguments focused on one nebula, the Andromeda Nebula in the constellation of Orion. By the end of the debate, however, the question remained unresolved, since no one could measure the distances to that or any other nebula.

Parallax measurements

Astronomers could measure the distances to stars – but only the nearest ones. The first person to do this was German astronomer Friedrich Bessel. In 1838, he used a phenomenon called parallax to work out the distance to a star called 61 Cygni. You can experience parallax by holding a finger in front of your

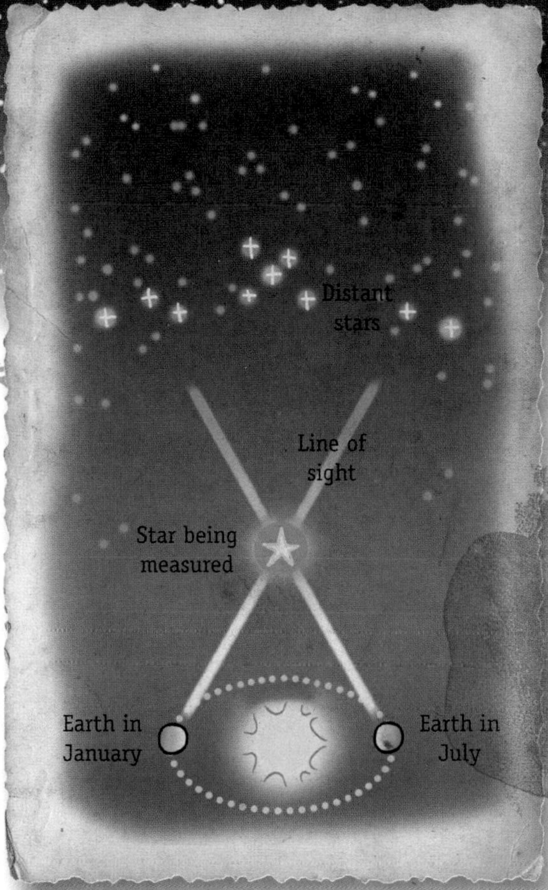

Above: The Andromeda Nebula. Left: Using parallax to find the distance of a nearby star, by measuring the star's position at different times of the year.

Diagram labels: Distant stars · Line of sight · Star being measured · Earth in January · Earth in July

face and closing one eye at a time. You will see the finger shift against the background; the nearer the finger, the greater the shift.

In the same way, 61 Cygni shifts its position against the background of more distant stars. But it is so far away that you can't detect the parallax by closing one eye at a time – your two viewpoints need to be much further apart. Thus Bessel observed the star on two occasions, six months apart, so that he was on opposite sides of Earth's orbit around the Sun each time – the equivalent to having eyes millions of kilometres apart. By then measuring how far the star appeared to shift against the background, he estimated the distance to 61 Cygni as 650,000 times that from Earth to the Sun – about 10 light years – very close to the actual figure.

The Cepheid yardstick

Parallax only works for the nearest stars, but in the early 20th century astronomers found a new way to measure distances in space. In 1908, US astronomer Henrietta Leavitt was studying a type of variable star called a Cepheid variable, found all over the night

Friedrich Bessel, the first to find out how far away the stars are

sky. Variable stars repeatedly become brighter then dimmer again over a set period, ranging from a few days to several weeks. Leavitt noticed that there was a direct relationship between these stars' periods and the amount of light they emit.

If you know how much light a star emits, you can tell how far away it is by measuring how bright it is in the sky – the further away, the dimmer it will appear. Astronomers had measured the distances to the nearest Cepheid variables using parallax. So now, by comparing Cepheids at known distances with ones with the same period elsewhere, they could calculate distances to much more distant stars and nebulas.

In 1923, another US astronomer, Edwin Hubble, was working at the Hooker Telescope at Mount Wilson in California. Using the new

Henrietta Leavitt, who found a new way to measure distant objects in space.

method, he calculated the distance from Earth to Cepheid variables he had spotted in Andromeda and some other nebulas. He was amazed to find that they were millions of light years away – much further away than any of the individual stars in the night sky. Curtis was right: the Universe was far bigger than anyone had imagined and the Milky Way was just one of many galaxies.

The expanding universe

In 1929, Hubble made another discovery. He managed to measure the speeds of 46 galaxies, by observing the spectrum of the light each one gives out. When a light source is moving towards you, the light it emits shifts towards the blue end of the spectrum; when it is moving away from you, it shifts towards the red end. Hubble found that every one of the galaxies was 'red shifted'– in other words, every single galaxy was speeding away from Earth. Unless our planet lay at the centre of the Universe, there was only one explanation: the whole Universe is constantly expanding.

Below right: The most distant galaxies ever observed appear red in this modern photograph.

Gathering from afar

Like most large telescopes, the Hooker Telescope that Hubble used had a curved mirror to collect and focus light from space, rather than a lens. The bigger a telescope's mirror or lens, the sharper the image and the more light it collects, allowing astronomers to observe fainter objects. Attaching light-sensitive photographic plates to telescopes allows astronomers to make a permanent record of their observations. Combined with long exposure times, such plates can record objects that are far too faint to be seen just by looking through the telescope.

Edwin Hubble

An uncertain world

Weirdness on a small scale, as explained by:

Niels Bohr, predictor of fixed electron orbits

Max Planck and his quantum theory

Erwin Schrödinger's fuzzy orbitals

Niels Bohr and his wife Margrethe

Following the discovery of the electron and the atomic nucleus, scientists worked hard to find out how they fitted together to make atoms. By the end of the 1920s, their theories and experiments had led them to some very strange conclusions about how the world works at the smallest scale.

After Ernest Rutherford discovered the atomic nucleus – the concentration of positive charge at the centre of every atom – he imagined that an atom's electrons would be circling around it, like planets around the Sun. But there was a big problem with this idea: physicists knew that an electron travelling around in a circle would give out electro-magnetic radiation and lose energy; if it did that, it would gradually spiral in towards and stick to the nucleus.

In 1913, Danish physicist Niels Bohr suggested that electrons only had certain 'allowed' orbits and that when an electron lost energy it would not spiral downwards but 'jump' to another orbit. And even the atoms with the lowest energy would remain in a low-energy orbit, which Bohr called the 'ground state', and not fall into the nucleus.

Quantum leaps

Bohr borrowed his idea from a theory proposed by German physicist Max Planck in 1900. Planck had suggested something similar when he was trying to explain the light produced by hot objects – like the orange glow of lava in a volcano. The only way he could make his equations match observations was by assuming that energy is 'quantised' – that electrons could gain or lose energy only in distinct steps, or quantum leaps, rather than steadily.

Planck wasn't sure his radical suggestion could be true, but in 1905 Albert Einstein used the idea to make sense of another effect, in which light can 'kick' electrons out of their atoms. Einstein supposed that light exists as packets of energy called 'photons' – and could no longer be thought of as a ripple travelling through space. No one else seemed convinced by these ideas, but they all fitted together neatly and matched both observable experience and mathematical calculations.

Artist's impression of Bohr's idea of atomic structure. Electrons orbit the nucleus only at certain distances, with definite energies.

Bohr's idea also explained why each element produces a particular spectrum of light when heated, as Bunsen and Kirchhoff had found in 1860. When atoms receive extra energy, from heat or electricity, their electrons jump to higher-energy orbits. When they 'fall' back down again, they emit light; the colour of the light depends upon the difference in energy between the levels – and that varies from element to element.

A perfect fit

In the 1920s, things became even weirder. By then, scientists had found enough evidence to

Max Planck, whose idea of 'quantised' levels of energy matched the behaviour of electrons in atoms

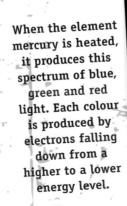

When the element mercury is heated, it produces this spectrum of blue, green and red light. Each colour is produced by electrons falling down from a higher to a lower energy level.

convince them that Einstein was right about light: it really is made of photons. But light also still behaved like waves – bizarrely, it was both a wave and a particle at the same time.

In 1923, French physicist Louis de Broglie wondered whether it might also work the other way round: that particles like the electron might also behave as waves. Putting de Broglie's idea into an equation immediately made perfect sense of Bohr's electron orbits: the only orbits allowed were those into which the electron 'waves' fitted perfectly. It was as if the electrons were vibrating guitar strings wrapped around the atom.

Fuzzy orbitals

Things then got more bizarre. In 1926, Austrian physicist Erwin Schrödinger worked out an equation that could describe the wavy behaviour of electrons. It predicted Bohr's energy levels perfectly. But rather than predicting where an electron was at any time, the equation could only determine the chance, or probability, that an electron would be in a particular place at a particular time. Bohr's

Using hugely complicated equations, Schrödinger finally got the point about particles behaving like waves.

well-defined orbits became fuzzy 'orbitals'. Schrödinger had uncovered a deep truth about the world at the smallest scale: all particles of matter are governed by 'waves of probability'.

Attempts to interpret Schrödinger's equation have confused physicists ever since. No one knows quite what the waviness of particles and the particleness of waves really mean. But the equations of quantum physics are extremely precise and successful in predicting and describing the behaviour of atoms and electrons. And without quantum physics, the digital revolution would never have happened, for the behaviour of electrons in the tiny integrated circuits upon which computers depend was only made possible by the discovery of quantum physics. Lasers, too, could only have been invented using the equations of quantum physics.

As waves, electrons fit perfectly around the orbits suggested by Bohr.

The particle ZOO

Discovering subatomic surprises in a hidden world, led by:

Paul Dirac and his antiparticles

Carl Anderson, discoverer of the positron

Hideki Yukawa and the strong interaction

John Cockcroft and **Ernest Walton**, who unleashed nuclear energy

The new theories of special relativity and quantum physics gave scientists new insight into a world we can never experience directly: the world of particles smaller than atoms – subatomic particles. The new theories of physics were uncovering a busy, energetic and unseen world.

In 1931, English physicist Paul Dirac combined all the equations of quantum physics with the equations of Einstein's relativity into one new equation – and discovered a whole new set of particles. Dirac's equation suggested that for every type of particle there is an 'antiparticle', with the same mass but opposite electric charge. In particular, Dirac predicted the existence of positively charged 'anti-electrons', which he called positrons.

Incredibly, Dirac was proved right when American physicist Carl Anderson discovered the positron just a year later. Anderson made his discovery in a cloud chamber, a tank filled with vapour in which particles leave tracks, just like aeroplanes leave vapour trails high in a clear blue sky. Magnetic and electric fields in the chamber make charged particles bend, and scientists can tell the mass and the electric charge from how much and which way the tracks bend.

Above: The international radiation symbol. Left: A nuclear power station.

Invisible forces

The positron was the first of a whole new 'zoo' of subatomic particles that scientists discovered, starting in the 1930s. Anderson himself discovered another particle in 1936, which turned out to be a heavy version of the electron – 200 times as massive – called the muon. Anderson had been searching for a different particle altogether, the meson, whose existence had been predicted by Japanese physicist Hideki Yukawa, in 1934.

Yukawa had suggested the meson to explain how the atomic nucleus holds together. He realised that a nucleus containing several protons would fly apart as a result of the repulsive force of the closely packed, positively charged protons – unless there was also a very strong force pulling them together. Yukawa worked out that the mystery force – today called the strong interaction – might be 'carried' by particles zipping to and fro between the protons and neutrons, and he worked out what mass those particles would have. The particle Yukawa predicted was eventually found in 1947. Another force that affects the particles in the atomic nucleus – called the weak interaction – was also predicted in the 1930s, and the subatomic particles that carry it were identified in the 1960s and 1970s.

Particle accelerators

Scientists have discovered hundreds of different particles, each with a different combination of mass and charge, in particle accelerators – machines that smash particles into each other at high speed. The first particle accelerator was built in 1929, by English physicist John Cockcroft and Irish physicist Ernest Walton. In 1932, newspapers worldwide reported that they had 'split the atom'. In fact, they had 'split the nucleus'. Cockcroft and Walton smashed protons at high speed into a tiny target made of lithium. Whenever a proton hit the nucleus of a lithium atom, it made the nucleus split in two, and the fragments hit a zinc sulphide screen, where they caused a tiny flash of light.

A positron bending in a magnetic field in Carl Anderson's cloud chamber, 1932.

Hideki Yukawa → was drawn to the idea of a strong force holding nuclei together.

Nuclear power

Experiments with elements with larger nuclei in the 1930s led to the invention of nuclear fission – the reaction that produces the energy in nuclear power stations and nuclear weapons. Uranium has the largest nucleus of any naturally occurring element, and one version of it has an unstable nucleus that makes it ideal for use in nuclear fission. In a fission reaction, large nuclei disintegrate, splitting into two and releasing energy. The nuclei also release neutrons when they disintegrate, and these neutrons can cause other nuclei to disintegrate, too. Under the right conditions, and if there is enough uranium in one place, this process can become a 'chain reaction'. In a nuclear power station, the chain reaction is carefully controlled – but in a nuclear bomb, it is not.

Cockcroft and Walton get set to switch on their particle accelerator and smash some atoms!

Cockcroft and Walton's experiment released energy from the nucleus – there was more energy after the experiment than before it. This 'extra' energy could be accounted for as a loss of mass: the total mass of fragments of nucleus left after the collision was less than the mass of the lithium nucleus before.

It was the first proof of Einstein's equation, $E = mc^2$, since the amount of extra energy was equal to the amount of mass lost multiplied by the square of the speed of light. And it was the first evidence that the mass-energy hidden in the nucleus could be harnessed.

Using just a few kilograms of uranium or plutonium, an atomic bomb can release as much energy as many thousands of tonnes of conventional explosives.

It's in the genes

Unlocking the code of life, with keys supplied by:

Friedrich Miescher, discoverer of DNA

Frederick Griffith and the transforming principle

Rosalind Franklin and X-ray diffraction

James Watson and **Francis Crick** and the double helix

A t the same time as physicists were uncovering a wealth of subatomic particles, biochemists – scientists studying the chemical reactions in living things – were working hard to discover exactly how genes can carry information from generation to generation. The key lay in a chemical compound called DNA.

DNA, deoxyribonucleic acid, was discovered in 1869, by Swiss biologist Friedrich Miescher, while he was trying to find out the chemical composition of the nucleus of human cells. Miescher found a way to extract the chemicals from the nuclei of white blood cells. These cells are found in abundance in pus, so he got hold

Friedrich Miescher discovered a very important chemical compound in cell nuclei.

of soiled bandages from a hospital. When Miescher analysed the contents of the cell nucleus, he found mostly proteins, as expected, but also a compound that was not a protein. It was slightly acidic in water and it contained large amounts of phosphorus. Unsure what it was, Miescher called it 'nuclein', but when it was purified – separated from the protein it clings onto – scientists began calling it nucleic acid. Its role in carrying genetic information would not become clear for more than 70 years.

Protein production line

In the early 20th century, scientists discovered that genes are carried on the chromosomes in

An artist's impression of a chromosome – a single length of DNA coiled around proteins.

One chromosome carries hundreds or even thousands of genes.

and that the instructions to build proteins must be the genetic instructions carried on the chromosomes.

Bearing the message

The discovery of DNA's role in carrying that information began in 1928. English micro-biologist Frederick Griffith was trying to make a vaccine to prevent the disease pneumonia. In his experiment, one type of bacterium gained the characteristics of another type – genetic information had passed from one species to the other in a chemical that Griffith called a 'transforming principle'. Meanwhile,

the nucleus of every cell. They realised there must be thousands of genes, and that together, they must carry instructions for hair colour, skin colour – in fact, all of the characteristics of a living thing. The chromosomes, then, were like an instruction manual for how to build a life form. But how could an instruction manual be written inside a cell nucleus?

Since the mid-19th century, chemists had known that living things are composed mostly of chemical compounds called proteins. There are millions of different types of proteins, including keratin, the main ingredient of hair and nails, and many are found inside cells. By the 1920s, biochemists worked out that proteins must be 'constructed' inside cells,

A model of a molecule of a protein called haemoglobin. The grey balls are carbon atoms.

Cell proteins

A living cell is like a bag in which countless chemical reactions happen. The bag, or 'membrane', is mostly fat, but the chemicals inside the cell are mainly proteins. Proteins are carbon-based, or 'organic', molecules. Carbon atoms join, or 'bond', together to make long chains and rings, and that is why there is such a huge variety of proteins.

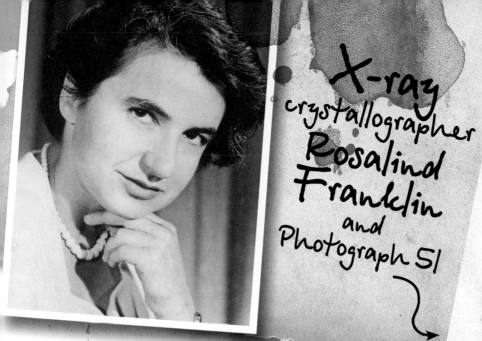

X-ray crystallographer Rosalind Franklin and Photograph 51

in 1933, Belgian chemist Jean Brachet found that DNA was present in the chromosomes inside the nucleus. And in 1943, after ten years of painstaking work, a team led by Canadian medical researcher Oswald Avery proved that DNA and Griffith's transforming principle were one and the same.

It followed that if scientists could work out the structure of the DNA molecule, they might be able to work out how DNA carries genetic information. Chemical analysis showed that DNA is made of several different parts: a kind of sugar called deoxyribose; phosphoric acid (phosphate); and four chemicals called 'bases'. The four bases are called adenine (A), thymine (T), guanine (G) and cytosine (C). Scientists noticed that in any sample of DNA, the amount of A was always the same as the amount of T, and the amount of G was the same as the amount of C. But trying to work out how the sugar, the phosphate and the bases fitted together proved challenging.

What the dots said

In the late 1940s, scientists had begun using a technique called X-ray diffraction to work out the structure of organic molecules. Bombard a crystal with X-ray, and the X-rays bounce off

Photograph 51 was taken by Rosalind Franklin in 1952. The dots were produced by X-rays that had bounced off atoms in DNA molecules. The dots' positions provided clues to the structure of DNA.

atoms, forming patterns of dots on a light-sensitive photographic film. It is then possible to work out the arrangement of the atoms from the pattern of dots. This is fairly easy with substances like minerals, which have a very regular crystal structure. But it is more difficult in large organic molecules like DNA, because they often form long fibres rather than crystals, and the arrangement of their atoms can be very complicated.

In 1951, New Zealand-born physicist Maurice Wilkins managed to obtain some X-ray diffraction results for DNA, which indicated that the DNA molecule must be a 'helix' – a shape like a coiled spring. Wilkins' colleague, English physicist Rosalind Franklin, carried out more X-ray diffraction, and in 1952, she produced a clear pattern of dots. Meanwhile, US molecular biologist James Watson and English molecular biologist Francis Crick were desperately trying to work out the structure of DNA before anyone else. After

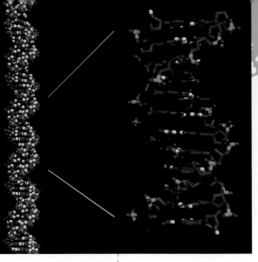

Right: A DNA string from a chromosome. Far right: An enlarged molecular model of the double helix.

Watson and Crick saw Franklin's photograph, they were able to build a model of DNA in their laboratory, in 1953.

Instructions included

Watson and Crick worked out that DNA is a double helix – like a spiral staircase. The sugar and phosphate form the twisting 'backbone' of the molecule, and the four bases are attached at regular intervals along it, like the steps of a staircase. The bases connect together in pairs – A joins to T, and C to G – which explained why there were always the same amounts of A and T, and C and G, in DNA samples.

A chromosome is a molecule of DNA wound around blobs of protein called histone. The 'base pairs' along the molecule are the letters of the code of life: they spell out the genetic information carried in genes, in the form of instructions for building proteins. Inside the cell nucleus, the double helix unwinds and sends copies of genes into the cell. Proteins called ribosomes read the code from the gene copies, and build proteins. This amazing process is going on millions of times, right now, inside (almost) every cell in your body.

Crick and watson's DIY DNA model

A cross-section of a cell nucleus and, at right, a close-up of a chromosome and the double-helix structure inside.

The origin of our species

Locating the starting point of the human race, with:

Charles Darwin and his theories of human evolution

Raymond Dart, finder of the Taung Child

Louis and **Mary Leakey** and the first ape-man fossil

Six years after Watson and Crick worked out the structure of DNA, in 1959, scientists searching for fossils found a skull of a distant human ancestor. It was then the oldest skull of a human ancestor ever found – and it suggested that humans emerged in Africa.

In 1871, Charles Darwin published a book about human evolution, *The Descent of Man*, in which he made a prediction: that fossils of human ancestors might be found in Africa, because that was the natural environment of the animals he believed to be our nearest relatives: gorillas and chimpanzees.

Despite the similarities between humans and apes, many people ridiculed Darwin's ideas. Some were holding onto an old idea that our species is completely separate from the animal kingdom, and were horrified by the idea of having apes as ancestors. It was true that there was then no fossil evidence to show the development of species from ape to human, so scientists with a special interest in human-like fossils – known as palaeoanthropologists – began looking for the 'missing links'.

Fossils found

Even most people who did believe that humans evolved from apes disagreed with Darwin about where our species originated. Palaeoanthropologists had found fossils of

Darwin as half-man, half-ape in an 1871 cartoon

'Neanderthals' in Europe and other possible human fossils in Indonesia (1891) and China (1923). But then, in 1924, Australian anatomist Raymond Dart found the fossilised skeleton of a young human-like creature in South Africa (later called the Taung Child). Dart was sure this was a missing link: it had a small skull like an ape, but the position of the hole in the base of the skull suggested it would have walked upright.

Few other people were convinced, even after several other fossil skulls and bones were found in Africa that seemed to be from human ancestors. Nevertheless, English palaeoanthropologists Louis and Mary Leakey travelled repeatedly to Africa to look for traces of our ancestors, and in 1959, after 20 years

Above left: Raymond Dart with the Taung Child. Above right: Louis and Mary Leakey examining some of their finds.

of searching, they found a remarkable fossil in Olduvai Gorge in Tanzania (in East Africa's Great Rift Valley). It was part of the skull of an 'ape-man', who would have walked upright and had a small brain and, based on evidence found nearby, used simple stone tools.

Fortunately, a new method of dating rocks, known as potassium-argon dating, had just been invented. The Leakeys' specimen was dated to nearly 2 million years old. Thereafter, people began to accept that our species may have evolved in Africa, and, since then, many other human fossils have been found in Africa, including some dating back 4.4 million years.

DNA evidence

It's not only fossils that tell us about our ancestors. Recently, studies of our DNA have shown that modern humans originated around 200,000 years ago and that the Neanderthals and the human-like species found in Indonesia and China are not our direct ancestors – they are from a separate branch of the evolutionary tree. But we do share an ancestor with them, which lived around a million years ago. And we share a common ancestor with chimpanzees: an animal that lived 7 million years ago.

Many questions about human evolution remain unanswered. But one thing seems certain: if you could go back far enough in your family tree, you would find an ape, in Africa – just as Darwin suggested.

About 4 million years ago, walking on two legs instead of four really got you noticed.

Episode **25**

A moving idea

Working out how mountains and oceans are made, in the company of:

Alfred Wegener, proponent of the theory of continental drift

Arthur Holmes, who identified the cause of the drift

Harry Hess, who described its effects

Most of the fossil finds of our ancestors in Africa have been found in the Great Rift Valley, a flat-bottomed valley that runs for thousands of kilometres through East Africa. According to a theory called plate tectonics, this valley will one day be an ocean.

In 1962, American geologist Harry Hess wrote a scientific report called *The History of Ocean Basins*, in which he outlined a theory about the ocean floor. Hess suggested that new rocks are constantly being formed where molten rock rises up through cracks in the seafloor, and that these new rocks steadily push the old seafloor outwards on either side

Harry Hess explaining his theory. The drawing shows seafloor spreading pushing continents away from each other.

of the cracks. Hess's theory, called 'seafloor spreading', gave new support to an old idea most geologists had rejected for 50 years.

A continental puzzle

In 1912, German geologist and explorer Alfred Wegener had proposed that Earth's continents are always moving. Moreover, he suggested that the continents were once joined together in a single supercontinent, and had been drifting apart ever since. This idea made sense of the fact that on the world map the continents seem to fit together like a badly made jigsaw puzzle. It also explained the fact that very similar fossils had been found in

'If mantle convection were accepted, a rather reasonable story could be constructed to describe the evolution of ocean basins and the waters within them.' HARRY HESS, 1962

Wegener piecing together the puzzle of continental drift

parts of the world separated by vast oceans and why there are matching rock types on opposite sides of wide oceans.

In 1929, English geologist Arthur Holmes explored how Wegener's 'continental drift' might happen. Beneath the solid outer layer of our planet (the crust), there is a huge layer of molten rock (the mantle). Holmes surmised that hot liquid rock rising to the surface of the mantle could split a continent and push the fragments apart. This rising of hot liquids is called convection. Holmes thought of it as a conveyor belt: when the molten rock cools, it falls back into the mantle; together the rising and falling currents form a 'convection cycle'.

Plate movements

Harry Hess had access to additional information that hadn't been available to Holmes, and it told him Holmes was right. In particular, Hess had maps of the ocean floor that revealed that there is a long mountain range running through the middle of each major ocean bed, like a great scar in Earth's crust. And he had records of the temperature of the crust on the ocean floor, which showed that the rocks along these 'mid-ocean ridges' were much warmer than the rest of the ocean.

The idea of convection cycles in the mantle also helped explain the origins of earthquakes and volcanoes. For as well as rising up through the mantle to the surface, rock is also pulled back down from the surface into the mantle.

As well as seafloor spreading, convection has other effects, some of which are shown below.

Subduction: one plate forced under another

Mid-ocean ridge: molten rock rising through crack

Hotspot volcanoes: where molten rock pierces crust

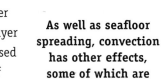

Coloured bands show the even spread of changes in magnetic field on either side of the Atlantic Ocean's mid-ocean ridge.

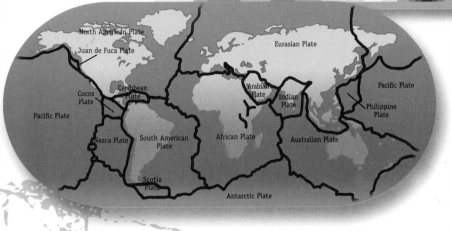

A map of the present-day tectonic plate boundaries.

Solid evidence

Hess's theory thus appeared to explain Wegener's continental drift, the young age of the ocean floor, and volcanoes and earthquakes. To prove Hess's theory one way or another, in 1963 scientists came up with a test. Geologists knew that Earth's magnetic field shifts over long periods, and the changes would be preserved in rocks – in molten rock, magnetic particles are free to line up with the Earth's magnetic field but in solid rock they can no longer move. If Hess's theory were correct, the record of the changes of the magnetic field would be the same on either side of the mid-ocean ridges. In the late 1960s, magnetic surveys of the ocean floor found just that.

An everchanging scene

Today, the theory of continental drift is known as plate tectonics. Our planet's crust is like a cracked eggshell, and each of the pieces is called a 'plate'. Most plates carry a continent and, at the boundaries where plates meet, ocean crust is either being made, by seafloor spreading, or destroyed by subduction.

Sometimes, a crack will appear within a plate, making a new plate boundary. This is what is happening in the Great Rift Valley in Africa. It is part of a fracture that is splitting the African plate. In a few million years, it will be hundreds of kilometres wide – and flooded with water from the Indian Ocean.

This process is called 'subduction', and it happens where ocean crust meets a continent. The thinner ocean crust is forced down under the thicker continental crust, and, as they grind together, the friction creates heat and vibration. The movement is not smooth: strain builds up, and is released in bursts that we experience as earthquakes. The heat melts rocks deep underground and some of this molten rock pushes its way up through the crust and, occasionally, breaks through to the surface, creating volcanoes. At the same time, the crumpling together of the plates pushes land upwards, forming mountain ranges.

Rift valley: continental plates pulling apart

Mountain building: two plates colliding

Whispers from the Universe

Looking back to the very beginning, alongside:

Georges Lemaître, who saw a 'primeval atom'

Fred Hoyle, who preferred the 'steady-state' theory

Arno Penzias and **Robert Wilson**,
discoverers of cosmic background radiation

Georges Lemaître, who used maths to suggest that space might be expanding.

Three years after Harry Hess published his theory about the spreading of the seafloor, a team of scientists led by US physicist Robert Dicke set out to search for a faint radio signal, coming from space, that they believed would help them understand the origin of the Universe. The signal turned out to be there – but it wasn't them who found it.

Dicke and his team were trying to test a theory formulated earlier by Belgian priest and astronomer Georges Lemaître. In 1927, Lemaître used the equations of Einstein's General Theory of Relativity to see what they might tell him about how the Universe alters over time. His results suggested that the Universe might be expanding. Two years later, the observation of astronomer Edwin Hubble that the galaxies are rushing away from each other seemed to confirm that idea. Another two years later, Lemaître realised that if you could run time backwards, an expanding Universe would be a shrinking one; therefore, at the beginning of time, the Universe would have been very, very small – a state Lemaître called the 'primeval atom'.

Two scenarios

In the 1940s, English astronomer Fred Hoyle came up with a different theory. He suggested that the Universe had existed forever and had no beginning. To make sense of this, Hoyle claimed that new matter was created all the time, everywhere, rather than all in one go just after the beginning of time. In 1949, while explaining this 'steady-state' theory, he used the term 'big bang' to describe Lemaître's theory. The name stuck: Lemaître's primeval atom became 'the Big Bang'.

Lemaître's theory suggested that the Universe had a beginning; Hoyle's suggested that it didn't. Using quantum physics and the current understanding of nuclear reactions, both theories could account for protons, neutrons and electrons combining to form simple elements such as hydrogen and helium. Both could also explain the formation of larger elements from hydrogen and helium, inside stars. For a while, both seemed likely. What was needed was a test to decide between them.

Fred Hoyle, whose 'steady-state' theory did not predict cosmic background radiation.

Cosmic radiation

If the Big Bang theory was right, then when the Universe was very young it would have been very small and very hot. It should

therefore be possible to detect some of the energy of the early Universe as electromagnetic radiation. Cosmic radiation – a whisper of the heat energy of the early Universe – is what Dicke and his team were looking for in 1965. But no sooner did they start their search than two other scientists nearby found it, quite by accident.

A year earlier, physicist Arno Penzias and astronomer Robert Wilson had started working at a radio antenna in New Jersey, hoping to detect radio waves from dust and gas around our galaxy. Penzias and Wilson found that their sensitive antenna was picking up an annoying 'radio noise' – seemingly random microwave radiation. They set about trying to work out where it was coming from, so that they could take it into account in their observations of space. They eliminated every source of microwave radiation they could think of: the atmosphere, the Sun, planet Jupiter, radar systems and radio broadcasts on Earth – they even removed pigeons and their droppings

Penzias and Wilson went to extreme lengths to limit interference.

Left: An image of the distribution of the cosmic background radiation across the whole sky, showing that there were very slight variations in temperature in the early Universe.

still fits with the predictions of the theory of the Big Bang. The theory has been tested in other ways, too. For example, it accurately predicts the proportion of hydrogen to helium that would have existed in the very early Universe. And experiments with subatomic particles in huge particle accelerators have managed to replicate the extreme conditions that would have existed in a tiny, hot, dense, young Universe.

There is still much more to find out and work out in cosmology, the study of the origins of our Universe. And while the Big Bang theory does a very good job of explaining the creation of matter and the expansion of the Universe, it cannot explain where the 'primeval atom' came from, nor can it explain why the laws of nature are what they are. Nevertheless, the latest observations and measurements from space all strongly suggest that the Big Bang theory is correct. And so it seems that our Universe began about 13.7 billion years ago as a very tiny, very dense, very hot speck of mass-energy.

from the antenna. Finally, they realised that the signal really *was* coming from outer space.

In fact, the radio noise was coming from every part of space, at all times of the day. The two scientists monitored it for a whole year – and it still stayed the same. They were baffled. But then they found out what Dicke and his team were looking for, and they realised at once that they had already found it – the cosmic radiation that would provide evidence in favour of the Big Bang theory.

Testing the theory

Since 1965, the 'cosmic background radiation' that Penzias and Wilson found has been studied in ever greater detail, and it

Timeline of the Universe, showing the Big Bang and the expansion of the universe over 13.7 billion years

Science and progress

Continuing the quest for knowledge — with a new generation of scientists

Modern body scans provide clear images of bones and internal organs.

The story of science doesn't end with the Big Bang. Scientists will continue to come up with new theories – and experiments to test them. And new scientific discoveries will find their way into our lives in more and more ways, through technology.

Many people think 'science' and 'technology' are more or less the same thing. But they are not. Science is a method of finding out why the world is the way it is, using observation, theory and experiment. Technology is 'know-how': inventing things, building things, using tools; and processes – like farming or mining.

So, while the history of science only really goes back to the 16th century, the history of technology stretches back much further – to the moment when our distant ancestors first made stone tools, about 2.5 million years ago. For a long time, technology progressed without any input from science. For example, ancient engineers built sewage systems that improved public health, without understanding the germ theory; selective breeding of farm animals happened for thousands of years before genetics; even the steam engine was

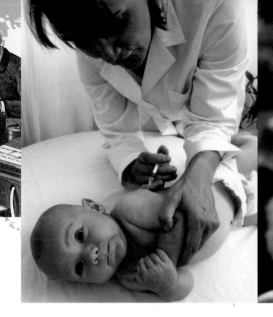

invented with almost no input from scientists. But when science did become closely involved with technology, the pace of technological change picked up.

Innovations and inventions

The first real impact of science in the history of technology was in the chemical industry, starting in the mid-19th century. Scientific understanding of chemical reactions led to the invention of artificial dyes, nitrogen-rich artificial fertilisers and synthetic materials such as plastics. The discoveries of electro-magnetism and electromagnetic radiation revolutionised communications, leading to the telegraph system then the telephone, radio and television. And by the 1930s, most houses in developed countries had an electricity supply that relied upon electromagnetic generators and electromagnetic transformers – and an understanding of electric circuits.

The germ theory of disease led to the development of safer surgery, antibiotics and other medicines. The discovery of the electron and quantum theory enabled the invention of the computer, the mobile phone and the Internet. And discoveries in geology helped energy companies to find and extract ever more oil to fuel it all.

Environmental concerns

One of the main consequences of the huge technological changes that have taken place has been a rapid increase in the world's

Above left: Chimpanzees use tools as our ape-like ancestors did. Above: Science led to vital inventions such as the telegraph. Above right: Vaccines have saved countless lives.

population: it was 2 billion in 1927, and reached 7 billion in 2011. Vaccines and other medicines have prevented millions of deaths. Artificial fertilisers and pesticides have enabled agricultural production to increase, to cope with all the extra mouths to feed. And better understanding of genetics has done the same, by enabling plant breeders to produce new crops with higher yields, better resistance to disease and shorter growing times.

In the 1960s and 1970s, many people began to question the science-driven technological progress that was taking place and, in particular, its effects on the environment. Toxic chemicals that do not exist in nature – the waste products of industrial processes – had found their way into rivers and seas. Huge swaths of forests had been cut down, to make way for agriculture, housing or industry for the growing population. Millions of tonnes of metal, plastics and other waste had found their way into landfill every year – and stayed there. And many species of plants and animals were becoming extinct because of the loss of their normal habitats.

Also of concern were accidents at nuclear power stations, which released radioactive substances into the environment, and the growing realisation that the burning of oil and coal were spreading huge amounts of carbon dioxide into the atmosphere. There is strong evidence that this has led to a rise in our planet's average temperature – 'global warming' – which may in turn cause disastrous rises in sea levels, melting of ice in polar regions and more frequent extreme weather such as hurricanes.

Science and technology may have helped cause these problems, but they also hold the solutions. Scientists and inventors can develop new low- or zero-carbon energy sources, make technology more energy-efficient, and use genetics to develop crops that make even better use of water or grow in more hostile environments.

Questions unanswered

In this brave new technological world, there is still a place for 'pure' science – asking questions about the world around us, for their own sake. And there are still many questions that remain unanswered. For example, biologists have a good idea of when life on Earth began – around 3.4 billion years ago –

**Above left: Soaring populations increase competition for limited resources.
Above: Global warming is melting ice caps, resulting in rising sea levels – and serious problems for polar bears.**

but they are still not sure exactly how it started. And cosmologists have worked out that the Universe began 13.7 billion years ago – but they don't know why.

Some of the biggest questions are in neuroscience, the study of our nerves and our brains. Neuroscientists have made great leaps forward in understanding individual brain cells (neurones) and their interconnections in the brain. But they have no idea how these connections make it possible for a brain to have curiosity – and to discover truths about the world through the process of observation, theory and experiment that we call science.

-- THE END --

Index

air
 atmospheric pressure, 12–13
 as elastic fluid, 23
 'fire air' (oxygen), 33
 'inflammable air' (hydrogen),
  32–33
 as particles, 22–23
 vacuums, 10–11
air pressure, 12–13
air resistance, 18
alchemy, 31–34
alpha rays, 62
amber, 24–25
Ampère, André, 42
Anderson, Carl, 76
Andromeda Nebula, 70
animalcules, 16
anthrax, 59
antibodies, 59
Aristotle
 on force and motion, 17–18
 on voids, 11
astronomy, 7–10, 70–72, 88–90
atmospheric pressure, 12–13
atomic bombs, 78
atomic nuclei see nucleus
atomic structures, 61–62, 73–75
atomic weights, 40, 54–55
atoms, 21, 40
Avery, Oswald, 81

bacteria, 57–59
barometers, 13
Bateson, William, 69
batteries, 38–39
Becquerel, Henri, 61, 62
Beijerinck, Martinus, 59
Bernoulli, Daniel, 23, 46
Bessel, Friedrich, 70–71
beta rays, 62
Bible, 36–37
'Big Bang', 89–90
Black, Joseph, 29–30
blood cells, 16
Boerhaave, Herman, 28
Bohr, Niels, 73
botany, 48
Boveri, Theodor, 68

Boyle, Robert, 12–13, 22–23, 31
Boyle's Law, 23
Brachet, Jean, 81
Brahe, Tycho, 9–10
Brand, Hennig, 32
Broglie, Louis de, 75
Bunsen, Robert, 53–54

caesium, 54
caloric, 30
carbolic acid (phenol), 59
carbon dioxide, 33
Carnot, Sadi, 44
Cartesian coordinates, 18
cathode ray tubes, 61
Catholic Church, 10
Cavendish, Henry, 33
cell proteins, 80
cell theory, 58
cells
 as basic unit of living things, 58
 blood cells, 16
 brain cells (neurones), 93
 chromosomes and, 68–69, 80
 skin cells, 58
Celsius, Anders, 29
Cepheid variables, 71–72
Chadwick, James, 62
chemistry as a science, 31–34
cholera, 59
chromosomes, 68, 80–82
Cockcroft, John, 77–78
compasses, 41–42
compound atoms, 41
conductors, 26
continental drift, 85–87
Copernicus, Nicolaus, 8–9
cosmic radiation, 89–90
cosmology, 88–90
Crick, Francis, 81–82
Curie, Marie, 61, 62
Curie, Pierre, 61, 62
Curtis, Heber, 72

Dalton, John, 40
Dart, Raymond, 84
Darwin, Charles, 47–49, 83–84
Davy, Humphry, 39
Democritus, 23
Desaguliers, John, 26
Descartes, René, 19

Dicke, Robert, 88
Dirac, Paul, 76
disease-causing pathogens,
 57–59
DNA (deoxyribonucleic acid)
 composition, 79–82
 discovery, 79–82
 and human origins, 84
 structure, 81–82

Earth see also geology
 as God's creation, 36–37
 Hutton's theory, 37
Earth-centred universe, 7–8
earthquakes, 86–87
Eddington, Arthur, 66
Einstein, Albert, 63–66, 74–75, 78
elastic fluids
 electricity, 24
 magnetism, 25
electric generators, 42–43
electric motors, 42
electric transformers, 43
electricity
 conductors and insulators, 26
 experiments with, 26–27
 as a fluid, 24–25, 27
 and magnetism, 41–43
 measuring strength of current,
  42
 origin of word, 25
 Volta's battery, 39
electromagnetic radiation, 52
electromagnetism, 41–43, 61
electromagnets, 42
electrons, 60–61, 73–75
elements
 four elements theory, 32
 light spectrum when heated, 74
 new discoveries, 53–55, 61
 periodic table, 55
$E=mc^2$, 65, 78
energy
 development of the concept,
  45–46
 and mass, 65
 mass-energy concept, 65, 78
 nuclear, 78
 quantised levels of, 74
environmental concerns, 92–93
evolution
 human, 83–84
 by natural selection, 47–49

role of genes and
 chromosomes, 68–69

Fahrenheit, Gabriel, 28–29
Faraday, Michael, 42, 52
fire see phlogiston theory
Fizeau, Hippolyte, 51
Flemming, Walther, 68
Franklin, Benjamin, 27
Franklin, Rosalind, 81–82
friction, 18
fuzzy orbitals, 75

galaxies, 70, 72
Galileo Galilei
 makes first thermometer, 28
 on motion and friction, 18
Galvani, Luigi, 39
galvanometers, 43
gamma rays, 52, 62
gases, 39–40
General Theory of Relativity,
 64–66
genes and genetics, 67–68, 79–82
genetic information, 79–82
geocentric universe, 7–8, 9
geology, 35–37, 85–87
germ theory of disease, 57–58
germs, 57
Gilbert, William, 24–25, 42
gravity, 19–20, 65
Gray, Stephen, 26
Great Rift Valley, 85, 87
Griffith, Frederick, 80
Guericke, Otto von, 11–12

Hales, Stephen, 23, 24
Hauksbee, Francis, 25
heat
 as fluid, 28–30
 latent, 29–30
 measurement, 28–29
 and 'motive power', 44
heliocentric universe, 8–10
helium, 54
Henry, Joseph, 42
heredity, laws of, 67–69
Herschel, William, 51
Hess, Harry, 85, 87
Holmes, Arthur, 86
Hooke, Robert, 12, 14–15
Hooker Telescope, 72
hospital hygiene, 56–58

Hoyle, Fred, 88–89
Hubble, Edwin, 72
human origins and evolution, 83–84
Hutton, James, 35–37
Huygens, Christiaan, 50
hydrogen, 33

ice calorimeter, 30
infrared radiation, 51
inheritance, 67–69
innovation and inventions, 92
insulators, 26
Ivanovsky, Dmitry, 59

Janssen, Pierre, 54
Johannsen, Wilhelm, 69
Joule, James, 45–46

Kepler, Johannes, 9–10
Kirchoff, Gustav, 53–54
Koch, Robert, 59

latent heat, 29–30
Lavoisier, Antoine
   heat as an element, 30
   'law of conservation of mass', 38–39
   pioneering chemical experiments, 34
'law of conservation of mass', 38–39
Leakey, Louis and Mary, 84
Leavitt, Henrietta, 71–72
Leeuwenhoek, Antony van, 16
Lemaître, Georges, 88
Leyden jars, 26
light
   as energy (photons), 74
   and magnetism, 52
   as spectrum of colours, 51–52, 75
   speed, 51–52, 63–65
   as stream of particles, 22, 50
   wave theory, 50
Linnaeus, Carl, 29, 47–48
Lister, Joseph, 59

magnetism, 24–25, 41–43, 52
mantle convection, 86
Marum, Martinus van, 26
mass-energy, 65
matter as tiny particles, 21–22, 40

Maxwell, James Clerk, 52, 63
Mendel, Gregor, 67–68, 69
Mendeleev, Dmitri, 555
mesons, 77
miasma theory of disease, 57
microorganisms, 16, 57
microscopes, 14–16
Miescher, Friedrich, 79
Minkowski, Hermann, 65
molecules, 40
Moon's orbit, 20
Morgan, Thomas Hunt, 69
motion
   and friction, 18
   Newton's three laws, 19–20
Müller, Hermann, 69
mutations, 69

natural selection, 47–49
nebulas, 72
neuroscience, 93
Newlands, John, 54–55
Newton, Isaac
   laws of force, motion and gravity, 18–20
   light as stream of particles, 22, 50
   particles of matter, 21–22
   theory of gravitation, 19–20
Nobel Prize, 62
Nollet, Abbé Jean-Antoine, 26–27
nuclear fission, 78
nucleus
   chromosomes in, 68
   cohesive forces, 77
   instability, 62, 78

ocean basins, 85–87
organic compounds, 54
Ørsted, Hans Christian, 41
oxygen, 33

parallax measurements, 70–71
particle accelerators, 77–78
particles
   and 'antiparticles', 76
   matter as, 21–22, 40
   subatomic, 76–77
   waviness of, 75
Pascal, Blaise, 12
Pasteur, Louis, 59–60
Penzias, Arno, 89–90
periodic table, 55

Philosopher's Stone, 32
phlogiston theory, 31–32, 34
phosphorous, 32
photons, 74
Planck, Max, 74
planetary orbits, 10, 17–20
planets, 7
plate tectonics, 85–87
Playfair, John, 37
positrons, 76
Priestley, Joseph, 33
Philosophiae Naturalis Principia Mathematica (Newton), 20
proteins, 80
protons, 62
Proust, Joseph, 40
Ptolemaic system, 7–8

quantum leaps, 74
quantum physics, 75

radio waves, 52
radioactivity, 61–62
radium, 61–62
relativity, 63–66
Remak, Robert, 57–58
Ritter, Johann, 51
Royal Society, 16
Rutherford, Ernest, 61, 62, 73

Scheele, Carl Wilhelm, 33
Schleiden, Matthias, 58
Schrödinger, Erwin, 75
Schwann, Theodor, 58
science versus technology, 91–92
seafloor spreading, 85, 87
sedimentary rocks, 36–37
Semmelweis, Ignaz, 56–57
Shapley, Harlow, 70
solar eclipse, 66
solenoids, 42
sound, 22
space
   measuring distances in, 70–72
   planetary system, 7–10
space-time, 63–65
species, their origin and evolution, 48–49
spectroscopes, 54
Stahl, Georg, 31–32
steam engines, 44–45
Sturgeon, William, 42
subatomic particles, 76–77

subduction, 86–87
Sun-centred universe, 8–10
Sutton, Walter, 68–69

telescopes, 9, 72
temperature scales, 29
thermodynamics, 46
thermometers, 28
Thompson, Benjamin (Count Rumford), 45
Thomson, JJ, 60–61, 62
time, relativity of, 65
Torricelli, Evangelista, 11–12
tuberculosis, 59

ultraviolet radiation, 51
universal laws, 20
Universe
   Earth-centred versus Sun-centred, 7–10
   expansion, 73, 88–90
   origins, 88–90
   size, 70–72
uranium, 61–62, 78
urea, 54
Ussher, James, 37

vaccines, 59
vacuum, 12–13
vacuum pumps, 12–13, 22
Villard, Paul, 62
viruses, 59
volcanoes, 36, 86–87
Volta, Alessandro, 39

Walton, Ernest, 77–78
Watson, James, 81–82
Wegener, Alfred, 85–86
Wilkins, Maurice, 81
Wilson, Robert, 89–90
Wöhler, Friedrich, 54

X-rays, 52

Yukawa, Hideki, 77

zoology, 48

> '*The greatest discoveries of science have always been those that forced us to rethink our beliefs about the universe and our place in it.*'
>
> US PHYSICIST
> ROBERT L PARK, 1999

Credits and Acknowledgments

Key

tl=top left; t=top; tc=top centre; tr=top right; cl=centre left; c=centre; cr=centre right; bl=bottom left; bc=bottom centre; bcl = bottom centre left; br=bottom right; bcr = bottom centre right; bg = background.

Photographs

Alamy 22tc, 28cl, 71bc; **Berenice Abbot/ Commerce Graphics** 50bl; **Bridgeman Art Library** 16tl, 25tc; **Caltech** 15c; **Getty Images** front cover bcr, cl, back cover cr, 4-5bc, 8bc, 9c, tl, 10bl, tl, 13cr, 16tc, 18tc, 18-19tc, 21cl, 22br, 24bl, 26tl, tr, 27cr, 29tr, 31bl, t, 32tl, 36tr, 37br, 38t, 39br, 40cr, 41br, 42c, 43br, cr, 44bc, cl, 45tl, 46bc, 47bc, bl, br, cr, 48bl, 49c, 52bc, 54bl, tl, 56cl, 57tc, 58b, cr, 60bl, 61t, 62cl, tr, 63bc, 66tr, 67t, 69bl, 70c, tr, 70-71t, 72br, tc, 73bl, 74bl, br, 76bl, 77br, 78br, 81tl, 82bc, 84tc, 87tr, 91bl, t, 92tl, tr; **iStockphoto.com** front cover bc, bg, back cover tl, endpapers, 6br, c, tr, 9br, 10bl, 11bc, 13tr, 15tc, 17t, 24cl, 24-25tr, 25c, cr, 28cr, 37bl, 40cr, 44-45tc, 46cl, 49tr, 54bl, 57tr, 59bc, 60cr, tl, 62bc, 66bl, 71cl, 72bl, tc, 76cl, 79t, 81tc, 82tr, 84tl, 92-93tc; **NASA** 4-5bg, 21t, 63t; **Shutterstock** front cover tl, spine tc, back cover tr, bg, 28t, 55br, 56t, 60t, 63cl, tr, 76t, 88cr, 93br; **Smithsonian Institute** 85cl; **Science Photo Library** front cover bcl, br, cr, tc, 4tl, 19br, 20bl, 30cr, 33tl, 34bc, 35cl, t, tr, 36c, 38bl, tr, 46cl, 48c, 53br, 54t, 55br, 57bc, 64-65bc, 73t, 74tr, 77tr, 79cr, 80tl, 81tr, 83cl, 84tl, 88bl, t, 89tc, 90tl, 92tc; **Science and Society Picture Library** 13bl; **Photolibrary** 4bg, 14bl, 14-15bg, tc; **Wikipedia** back cover tc, 5bg, 11br, 14c, 15cr, 30c, 35br, 50-51bg, 52tl, 67c, tl, 68-69tc, 69c, 79bc, 95br.

All repeated background images courtesy of Shutterstock.

Cartoon illustrations
Dave Smith/The Art Agency

Other illustrations
Dr Mark A Garlick 90br; Mick Posen/The Art Agency 18-19bc, 22bl, 27tr, 29r, 30br, 32tr, 36tl, 39tr, 46bl, 52tl, 62tl; Wildlife Art Ltd 86-87bc.